Informing the legislative debate since 1914

Cuba: U.S. Policy and Issues for the 113th Congress

Mark P. Sullivan
Specialist in Latin American Affairs

May 20, 2014

Congressional Research Service
7-5700
www.crs.gov
R43024

Summary

Cuba remains a one-party communist state with a poor record on human rights. The country's political succession in 2006 from the long-ruling Fidel Castro to his brother Raúl was characterized by a remarkable degree of stability. In February 2013, Castro was reappointed to a second five-year term as president (until 2018, when he would be 86 years old), and selected 52-year old former Education Minister Miguel Díaz-Canel as his First Vice President, making him the official successor in the event that Castro cannot serve out his term. Raúl Castro has implemented a number of gradual economic policy changes over the past several years, including an expansion of self-employment. A party congress held in April 2011 laid out numerous economic goals that, if implemented, could significantly alter Cuba's state-dominated economic model. Few observers, however, expect the government to ease its tight control over the political system. While the government reduced the number of political prisoners in 2010-2011, the number increased in 2012; moreover, short-term detentions and harassment have increased significantly over the past several years.

U.S. Policy

Congress has played an active role in shaping policy toward Cuba, including the enactment of legislation strengthening and at times easing various U.S. economic sanctions. While U.S. policy has consisted largely of isolating Cuba through economic sanctions, a second policy component has consisted of support measures for the Cuban people, including U.S. government-sponsored broadcasting (Radio and TV Martí) and support for human rights and democracy projects. The Obama Administration has continued this similar dual-track approach. While the Administration has lifted all restrictions on family travel and remittances, eased restrictions on other types of purposeful travel, and moved to reengage Cuba on several bilateral issues, it has also maintained most U.S. economic sanctions in place. On human rights, the Administration welcomed the release of many political prisoners in 2010 and 2011, but it has also criticized Cuba's continued harsh repression of political dissidents through thousands of short-term detentions and targeted violence. The Administration has continued to call for the release of U.S. government subcontractor Alan Gross, detained in 2009 and sentenced to 15 years in prison in 2011, and maintains that Gross's detention remains an impediment to more constructive relations.

Legislative Activity

Strong interest in Cuba is continuing in the 113th Congress with attention focused on economic and political developments, especially the human rights situation, and U.S. policy toward the island nation, including sanctions. The continued imprisonment of Alan Gross remains a key concern for many Members. In March 2013, Congress completed action on full-year FY2013 appropriations with the approval of H.R. 933 (P.L. 113-6), which continues to provide funding for Cuba democracy and human rights projects and Cuba broadcasting (Radio and TV Martí).

In January 2014, Congress completed action on FY2014 appropriations with the approval of an FY2014 omnibus appropriations measure, H.R. 3547 (P.L. 113-76), which continues funding for Cuba democracy and human rights projects and Cuba broadcasting. In the measure, Congress stated that up to $17.5 million in Economic Support Funds (ESF) should be made available for programs and activities in Cuba, but also stipulated that no ESF may be obligated by the U.S. Agency for International Development for any new programs or activities in Cuba. The State Department estimates that $20 million in ESF will be provided for Cuba democracy funding for

FY2014, and the Administration's request for FY2015 is for $20 million. For Cuba broadcasting, the FY2014 omnibus measure provided $27.043 million, and the FY2015 request is for $23.130 million. With regard to Cuba sanctions, both the House and Senate versions of the FY2014 Financial Services and General Government appropriations measure, H.R. 2786 and S. 1371, had different provisions that would have tightened and eased travel restrictions respectively, but none of these provisions were included in the FY2014 omnibus appropriations measure (P.L. 113-76).

Several other initiatives on Cuba have been introduced in the 113th Congress. Several would lift or ease U.S. economic sanctions on Cuba: H.R. 214 and H.R. 872 (overall embargo); H.R. 871 (travel); and H.R. 873 (travel and agricultural exports). H.R. 215 would allow Cubans to play organized professional baseball in the United States. H.R. 1917 would lift the embargo and extend nondiscriminatory trade treatment to the products of Cuba after Cuba releases Alan Gross from prison. Identical initiatives, H.R. 778/S. 647 would modify a 1998 trademark sanction; in contrast, H.R. 214, H.R. 872, H.R. 873, and H.R. 1917 each have a provision that would repeal the sanction. H.Res. 121 would honor the work of Cuban blogger Yoani Sánchez. H.Res. 262 would call for the immediate extradition or rendering of all U.S. fugitives from justices in Cuba.

This report will be updated periodically during the 113th Congress. For additional information, see CRS Report RL31139, *Cuba: U.S. Restrictions on Travel and Remittances*.

Contents

Figures

Appendixes

Contacts

Recent Developments

On May 5, 2014, the independent Havana-based Cuban Commission on Human Rights and National Reconciliation reported that there were 3,821 short-term detentions for political reasons in the first four months of 2014, far higher than the same period over the past several years. (See "Human Rights Conditions" below.)

On April 30, 2014, the State Department released *Country Reports on Terrorism 2013*, which noted that Cuba has long provided safe haven to members of the Basque Fatherland and Liberty (ETA) and the Revolutionary Armed Forces of Colombia (FARC), but that there was no indication that the Cuban government provided weapons or paramilitary training to terrorist groups. The report also noted that the Cuban government continued to harbor fugitives from U.S. justice. (See "Terrorism Issues" below.)

On April 3, 2014, an *Associated Press* investigative report alleged that the U.S. Agency for International Development (USAID) had established a "Cuban Twitter" known as ZunZuneo from 2010 to 2012 that was designed as a "covert" program "to undermine" Cuba's communist government. USAID strongly contested the facts presented in the report and asserted that it was not a covert program. (See "Oversight of U.S. Democracy Assistance to Cuba" below.)

On March 29, 2014, Cuba approved a new foreign investment law (to go into effect in 90 days) with the goal of attracting needed foreign capital to the country. While the law cuts taxes for foreign investors significantly, it remains to be seen to what extent the new law will actually attract investment. (See "Economic Conditions and Reform Efforts" below.)

During the second week of March 2014, the United States along with the Bahamas, Cuba, and Jamaica released a document known as the Wider Caribbean Region Multilateral Technical Operating Procedures for Offshore Oil Pollution Response (MTOP) that consists of information of what would need to be done and coordinated in the case of an oil spill. (See "Cuba's Offshore Oil Development" below.)

On March 6, 2014, the U.N. Security Council issued the Panel of Experts for North Korea report, which concluded that July 2013 attempted shipment of weapons to North Korea from Cuba that was intercepted by Panama were violations of U.N. sanctions banning weapons transfers to North Korea. The report maintained that there was a "clear and conscious intention to circumvent the [U.N. Security Council] resolutions." (See "North Korean Ship Incident" below.)

On February 28, 2014, the State Department released its 2014 International Narcotics Control Strategy Report, which noted that law enforcement communication with Cuba "gradually increased in frequency and transparency over the course of 2013, especially concerning efforts to target drug trafficking at sea." As in past years, the report noted that a bilateral counternarcotics accord could advance the efforts undertaken by both countries. (See "Anti-Drug Cooperation" below.)

On February 27, 2014, Fernando González—one of the "Cuban five" intelligence agents convicted in 2001 on espionage charges by a U.S. Federal Court—was released from prison after serving his sentence and swiftly returned to Cuba. Three of the "Cuban five" remain in the United States serving their sentences. (See "Cuban Five—Now Three" below.)

For developments earlier in 2013, see **Appendix B**.

Introduction

Political and economic developments in Cuba and U.S. policy toward the island nation, located just 90 miles from the United States, have been significant congressional concerns for many years. Since the end of the Cold War, Congress has played an active role in shaping U.S. policy toward Cuba, first with the enactment of the Cuban Democracy Act of 1992 (P.L. 102-484, Title XVII) and then with the Cuban Liberty and Democratic Solidarity Act of 1996 (P.L. 104-114). Both of these measures strengthened U.S. economic sanctions on Cuba that had first been imposed in the early 1960s, but the measures also provided roadmaps for a normalization of relations dependent upon significant political and economic changes in Cuba. A decade ago, Congress partially modified its sanctions-based policy toward Cuba when it enacted the Trade Sanctions Reform and Export Enhancement Act of 2000 (P.L. 106-387, Title IX) allowing for U.S. agricultural exports to Cuba that led to the United States becoming a major source for Cuba's food imports.

Over the past decade, much of the debate over U.S. policy in Congress has focused on U.S. sanctions, especially over U.S. restrictions on travel to Cuba. The George W. Bush Administration initially liberalized U.S. family travel to Cuba in 2003, but subsequently tightened restrictions on family and other categories of travel in 2004 because of Cuba's crackdown on political dissidents. In 2009, Congress took legislative action in an appropriations measure (P.L. 111-8) to ease restrictions on family travel and travel for the marketing of agricultural exports, marking the first congressional action easing Cuba sanctions in almost a decade. The Obama Administration took further action in April 2009 by lifting all restrictions on family travel and on cash remittances by family members to their relatives in Cuba and restarting semi-annual migration talks that had been curtailed in 2004. In January 2011, the Administration announced the further easing of restrictions on educational and religious travel to Cuba and on non-family remittances, and it also expanded eligible airports in the United States authorized to serve licensed charter flights to and from Cuba.

This report is divided into three major sections analyzing Cuba's political and economic situation, U.S. policy toward Cuba, and selected issues in U.S.-Cuban relations. The first section includes a brief historical political background on Cuba; a discussion on the current political situation under Raúl Castro, including human rights conditions; an examination of economic conditions and policy changes that have occurred to date under Raúl Castro; and Cuba's foreign relations. The second section on U.S. policy provides a broad overview of U.S. policy historically through the George W. Bush Administration and then a discussion of current policy under the Obama Administration. It then provides a brief discussion on the general policy debate regarding the direction of U.S. policy toward Cuba. The third section analyzes many of the key issues in U.S.-Cuban relations that have been at the forefront of the U.S. policy debate on Cuba and have often been the subject of legislative initiatives. While legislative initiatives are noted throughout the report where appropriate, a final section of the report provides a listing of current bills and resolutions introduced in the 113th Congress. An appendix also provides links to selected executive branch reports and web pages on Cuba.

Figure 1. Provincial Map of Cuba

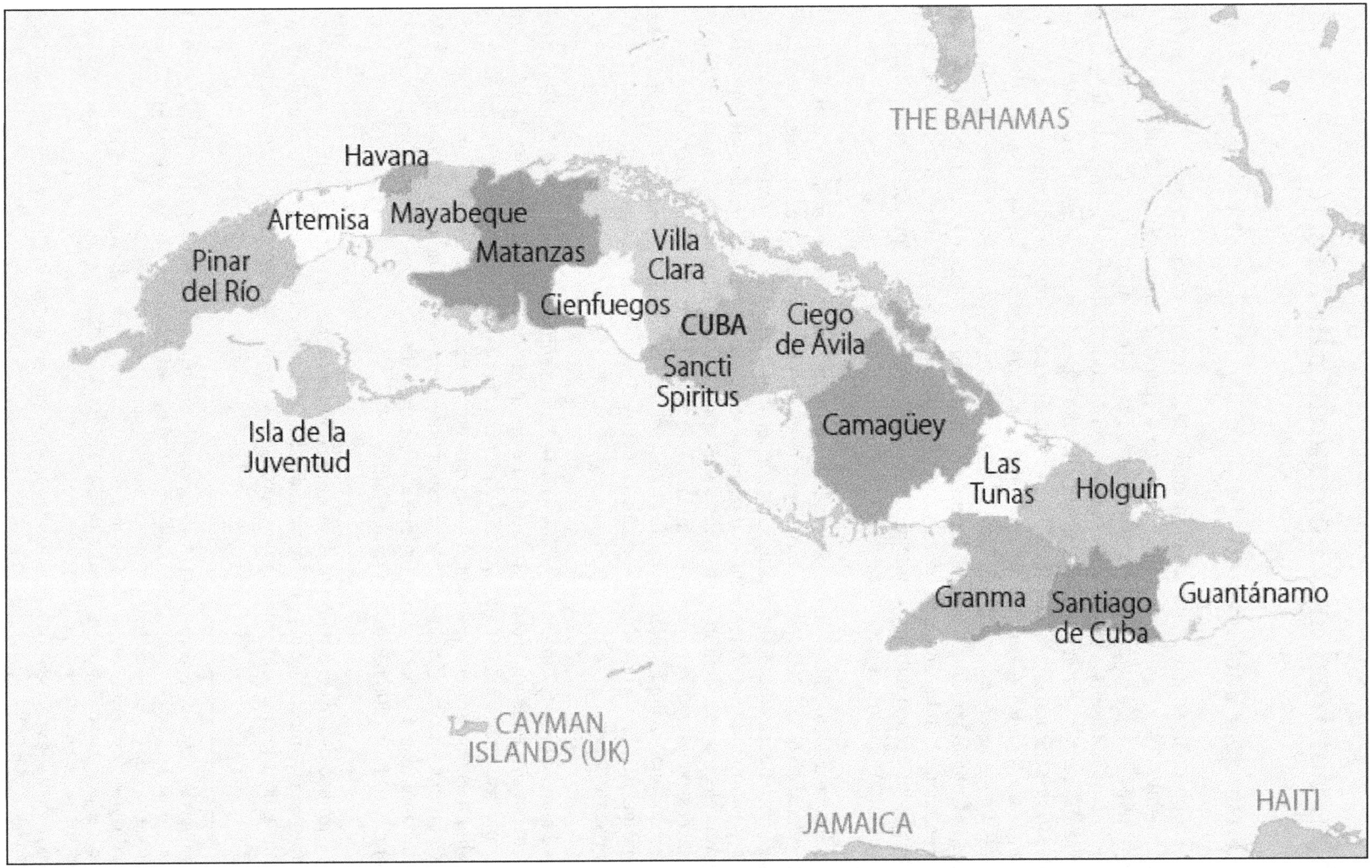

Source: CRS.

Notes: This maps shows 15 provinces and the special municipality of Isla de la Juventud. See a current interactive provincial map of Cuba, showing municipalities and other information, from *Juventud Rebelde* (Cuba), available at http://www.juventudrebelde.cu/multimedia/graficos/nueva-division-politico-administrival.

Cuba's Political and Economic Situation

Brief Historical Background[1]

Cuba did not become an independent nation until 1902. From its discovery by Columbus in 1492 until the Spanish-American War in 1898, Cuba was a Spanish colony. In the 19th century, the country became a major sugar producer with slaves from Africa arriving in increasing numbers to work the sugar plantations. The drive for independence from Spain grew stronger in the second half of the 19th century, but it only came about after the United States entered the conflict when the USS *Maine* sank in Havana Harbor after an explosion of undetermined origin. In the aftermath of the Spanish-American War, the United States ruled Cuba for four years until Cuba was granted its independence in 1902. Nevertheless, the United States still retained the right to intervene in Cuba to preserve Cuban independence and maintain stability in accordance with the Platt Amendment[2] that became part of the Cuban Constitution of 1901. The United States subsequently intervened militarily three times between 1906 and 1921 to restore order, but in 1934, the Platt Amendment was repealed.

Cuba's political system as an independent nation was often dominated by authoritarian figures. Gerardo Machado (1925-1933), who served two terms as president, became increasingly dictatorial until he was ousted by the military. A short-lived reformist government gave way to a series of governments that were dominated behind the scenes by military leader Fulgencio Batista until he was elected president in 1940. Batista was voted out of office in 1944 and was followed by two successive presidents in a democratic era that ultimately became characterized by corruption and increasing political violence. Batista seized power in a bloodless coup in 1952 and his rule progressed into a brutal dictatorship. This fueled popular unrest and set the stage for Fidel Castro's rise to power.

Castro led an unsuccessful attack on military barracks in Santiago, Cuba, on July 26, 1953. He was jailed, but subsequently freed and went into exile in Mexico where he formed the 26th of July Movement. Castro returned to Cuba in 1956 with the goal of overthrowing the Batista dictatorship. His revolutionary movement was based in the Sierra Maestra and joined with other resistance groups seeking Batista's ouster. Batista ultimately fled the country on January 1, 1959, leading to more than 45 years of rule under Fidel Castro until he stepped down from power provisionally in July 2006 because of poor health.

While Castro had promised a return to democratic constitutional rule when he first took power, he instead moved to consolidate his rule, repress dissent, and imprison or execute thousands of opponents. Under the new revolutionary government, Castro's supporters gradually displaced

---

[1] Portions of this background are drawn from U.S. Department of State, "Background Note: Cuba," April 28, 2011. For further background, see *Cuba, A Country Study*, ed. Rex A. Hudson, Federal Research Division, Library of Congress, (Washington, DC: U.S. Government Printing Office, 2002); "Country Profile: Cuba," Federal Research Division, Library of Congress, September 2006, available at http://lcweb2.loc.gov/frd/cs/profiles/Cuba.pdf; *Cuba, A Short History*, ed. Leslie Bethell (Cambridge University Press, 1993); and Hugh Thomas, *Cuba: The Pursuit of Freedom*, (New York, Harper & Row, Publishers, 1971).

[2] U.S. Senator Orville Platt introduced an amendment to an army appropriation bill that was approved by both houses and enacted into law in 1901.

members of less radical groups. Castro moved toward close relations with the Soviet Union while relations with the United States deteriorated rapidly as the Cuban government expropriated U.S. properties (see "Background on U.S.-Cuban Relations" below). In April 1961, Castro declared that the Cuban revolution was socialist, and in December 1961, he proclaimed himself to be a Marxist-Leninist. Over the next 30 years, Cuba was a close ally of the Soviet Union and depended on it for significant assistance until the dissolution of the Soviet Union in 1991.

From 1959 until 1976, Castro ruled by decree. In 1976, however, the Cuban government enacted a new Constitution setting forth the Cuban Communist Party (PCC) as the leading force in state and society, with power centered in a Political Bureau headed by Fidel Castro. Cuba's Constitution also outlined national, provincial, and local governmental structures. Since then, legislative authority has been vested in a National Assembly of People's Power that meets twice annually for brief periods. When the Assembly is not in session, a Council of State, elected by the Assembly, acts on its behalf. According to Cuba's Constitution, the president of the Council of State is the country's head of state and government. Executive power in Cuba is vested in a Council of Ministers, also headed by the country's head of state and government, that is, the president of the Council of State.

Fidel Castro served as head of state and government through his position as president of the Council of State from 1976 until February 2008. While he had provisionally stepped down from power in July 2006 because of poor health, Fidel still officially retained his position as head of state and government. National Assembly elections were held on January 20, 2008, and Fidel Castro was once again among the candidates elected to the now 614-member legislative body. (As in the past, voters were only offered a single slate of candidates.) On February 24, 2008, the new Assembly was scheduled to select from among its ranks the members of the Council of State and its president. Many observers had speculated that because of his poor health, Fidel would choose not to be reelected as president of the Council of State, which would confirm his official departure from heading the Cuban government. Statements from Castro himself in December 2007 hinted at his potential retirement. That proved true on February 19, 2008, when Fidel announced that he would not accept the position as president of the Council of State, essentially confirming his departure as titular head of the Cuban government.

Political Conditions

After Fidel stepped down from power, Cuba's political succession from Fidel to Raúl Castro was characterized by considerable stability. After two and one half years of provisionally serving as president, Raúl Castro officially became Cuba's president on February 24, 2008, when Cuba's legislature selected him as president of the 31-member Council of State.[3]

While it was not a surprise to observers for Raúl to succeed his brother Fidel officially as head of government, the selection of José Ramón Machado Ventura as the Council of State's first vice president in February 2008 was a surprise. Born in 1930, Machado was part of the older generation of so-called *históricos* of the 1959 Cuban revolution along with the Castro brothers (Fidel Castro was born in August 1926, while Raúl Castro was born in June 1931). Described as a

---

[3] For more on Cuba's political succession, see CRS Report RS22742, *Cuba's Political Succession: From Fidel to Raúl Castro.* For background discussion of potential Cuban political scenarios envisioned in the aftermath of Fidel Castro's stepping down from power in 2006, see CRS Report RL33622, *Cuba's Future Political Scenarios and U.S. Policy Approaches.*

hard-line communist party ideologue, Machado reportedly was a close friend and confident of Raúl for many years.[4] The position of first vice president of the Council of State is significant because, according to the Cuban Constitution, the person holding the office is the official successor to the president.

While Raúl Castro began implementing some economic reforms in 2008, there has been no change to his government's tight control over the political system and few observers expect there to be, with the government backed up by a strong security apparatus. Under Raúl, who served as defense minister from the beginning of the Cuban revolution until 2008, the Cuban military has played an increasing role in government with several key military officers and confidants of Raúl serving as ministers.

The Cuban Communist Party (PCC) held its sixth congress in April 2011. While the party concentrated on making changes to Cuba's economic model, some political changes also occurred. As expected, Fidel was officially replaced by Raúl as first secretary of the PCC, and First Vice President José Ramón Machado became the party's second secretary. The party's Political Bureau or Politburo was reduced from 23 to 15 members, with 3 new members, Marino Murrillo, Minister of Economy Adel Yzquierdo Rodriguez, and the first secretary of the party in Havana, Mercedes Lopez Acea. The party's Central Committee also was reduced from 125 to 115 members, with about 80 of those being new members of the committee.

At the April 2011 party congress, Raúl Castro proposed two five-year term limits for top positions in the party and in the government, calling for systematic rejuvenation, a change that was confirmed by a January 2012 national PCC conference. Cuba's revolutionary leadership has been criticized by many observers for remaining in party and government positions far too long, and for not passing leadership opportunities to a younger generation. Some observers had expected leadership changes and more significant reforms at the January 2012 PCC conference. While this did not occur, the PCC approved a resolution by which its Central Committee would be allowed to replace up to 20% of its 115 members within its five-year mandate.[5]

On February 3, 2013, Cuba held elections for over 600 members of the National Assembly of People's Power, the national legislature, as well as over 1,600 provincial government representatives, both for five-year terms. Under Cuba's one-party system, the overwhelming majority of those elected are PCC members. Critics maintain that elections in Cuba are a sham and entirely controlled by the PCC.

The new National Assembly met on February 24, 2013, to select the next president of the Council of State, Cuba's head of government. As expected, Raúl Castro was selected for a second five year-term as president (until February 2018, when Raúl will be 86 years old), but Castro also indicated that this would be his last term in conformity with the new two-term limit for top officials. Most significantly, First Vice President José Ramón Machado, 82 years old, was replaced by 52-year old Miguel Díaz-Canel Bermúdez, who was serving as one of the Council of State's vice presidents. Díaz-Canel's appointment as the official constitutional successor to President Castro represents a move toward bringing about generational change in Cuba's political

---

[4] Daniel Dombey, Richard Lapper, and Andrew Ward, "A Family Business, Cuban-Americans Look Beyond the Havana Handover," Financial Times, February 27, 2008.

[5] Juan O. Tamayo, "Cuban Communists OK Term Limits for Party and Government Officials," *Miami Herald*, January 29, 2012, and "Cuba's Communists Meet to Update Party, Not Much Buzz on Street," *Miami Herald*, January 28, 2012; Patricia Grogg, "Cuba: Party Aims for Efficient, Inclusive Socialism," *Inter Press Service*, February 1, 2012.

system. Díaz-Canel became a member of the Politburo in 2003 and also held top PCC positions in the provinces of Villa Clara and Holguín. He became education minister in 2009 until he was tapped to be a vice president of the Council of State. Díaz-Canel has been described in media reports as an experienced manager with good relations with the military and as someone that worked his way up through the party.[6]

In another significant move in February 2013, the National Assembly appointed Esteban Lazo Hernández as the new president of Cuba's National Assembly. Lazo, who is the Cuban government's highest ranking official of Afro-Cuban descent, replaced long-time National Assembly President Ricardo Alarcón, who was not a candidate in this year's National Assembly elections. Lazo has held top party positions in several provinces and has served as a vice president of the Council of State.

While generational change already appears to be underway in Cuba's political system, this does not signify an easing of Cuba's tightly controlled regime. In speaking on the 60th anniversary of the start of the Cuban revolution on July 26, 2013, President Castro asserted that a generational transfer of power had already begun, stating that "there is a slow and orderly transfer of the leadership of the revolution to the new generations."[7] Some observers maintain that while the leadership transition in 2018 (or earlier, given that Raúl Castro's is 82 years old) will likely be smooth, there is a greater likelihood for a growth in factionalism within the system without Castro at the helm.[8]

On September 15, 2013, Cuba's Conference of Catholic Bishops issued a pastoral letter maintaining that, just as economic changes were occurring, Cuba's political order also needed to be updated. The bishops maintained that there should be the right of diversity with respect to thought, creativity, and the search for truth, and maintained that out this diversity arises the need for dialogue among diverse social groups.[9] In his March 2012 pastoral visit to Cuba, Pope Benedict VI had urged Cubans "to build a renewed and open society."[10]

Human Rights Conditions

The Cuban government has a poor record on human rights, with the government sharply restricting freedoms of expression, association, assembly, movement, and other basic rights since the early years of the Cuban revolution. The government has continued to harass members of the Ladies in White (*Damas de Blanco*) human rights group that was formed in 2003 by the female relatives of the so-called "group of 75" dissidents arrested that year in a massive crackdown (for more, see text box below). Two Cuban political prisoners conducting hunger strikes have died in recent years, Orlando Zapata Tamayo in February 2010 and Wilman Villar Mendoza in January 2012. Tamayo died after an 85-day hunger strike that he had initiated to protest inhumane

---

[6] "Castro Dynasty Capped at 59 Years," Latin American Weekly Report, February 28, 2013; Damien Cave and Victoria Burnett, "As Castro Era Drifts to Close, A New Face Steps in at No. 2," *New York Times*, February 28, 2013; Marc Frank, "Castro Successor Lacks Charisma But Is Experienced Manager," *Reuters*, February 26, 2013.

[7] Marc Frank, "Cuba's Raúl Castro Promises Succession Has Started," *Reuters*, July 26, 2013.

[8] For example, see "Cuba Country Report," *Economist Intelligence Unit (EIU)*, September 2013, p. 3.

[9] Conferencia de Obispos Católicos de Cuba, "Carta Pastoral de los Obispos Católicos de Cuba, La Esperanza No Defrauda," (issued September 15, 2013), available at http://www.iglesiacubana.org/index.php?option= com_phocadownload&view=file&id=56&Itemid=108.

[10] See "March 2012 Visit of Pope Benedict" in CRS Report R41617, *Cuba: Issues for the 112th Congress*.

---

conditions in Cuba's prisons. Villar Mendoza died following a 50-day hunger strike after he was convicted of "contempt" of authority and sentenced to four years in prison.

Amnesty International (AI) published a report in March 2012 maintaining that "the Cuban government wages a permanent campaign of harassment and short-term detentions of political opponents to stop them from demanding respect for civil and political rights." The report maintained that the release of dozens of political prisoners in 2011 "did not herald a change in human rights policy." AI asserted that "the vast majority of those released were forced into exile, while in Cuba the authorities were determined to contain the dissidence and government critics with new tactics," including intimidation, harassment, surveillance, and "acts of repudiation," or demonstrations by government supporters targeting government critics.[11]

AI has called attention to several prisoners of conscience[12] in Cuba. These currently include Iván Fernández Depestre, convicted of "dangerousness" (a pre-emptive measure defined as the special proclivity of a person to commit crimes) in early August 2013 after participating in a peaceful protest and sentenced to three years in prison; and brothers Alexeis, Django, and Vianco Vargas Martín, members of the UNPACU, who were detained in late 2012 in Santiago and charged with using "violence or intimidation" against a state official. AI has also reported on other cases of arbitrary detention by the Cuban government, including the continued detention since March 2012 of Ladies in White member Sonia Garro Alfonso and her husband Ramón Alejandro Muñoz González (also see text box below on the Ladies in White).[13]

Beyond AI's more narrow definition of prisoners of conscience, the Cuban government holds a larger number of political prisoners, generally defined as a person imprisoned for his or her political activities. While the Cuban government released numerous political prisoners in recent years, including more than 125 released in 2010-2011 with the help of Cuba's Catholic Church, the number of political prisoners has reportedly increased since 2012, according to the Havana-based Cuban Commission on Human Rights and National Reconciliation (CCDHRN). In November 2013, the group estimated that Cuba held at least 87 political prisoners. This is up from an estimated 50 in April 2012, but less than the more than 200 estimated at the beginning of 2010.[14]

Short-term detentions for political reasons have increased significantly over the past several years, a reflection of the government's change of tactics in repressing dissent. The CCDHRN reports that there were at least 2,074 such detentions in 2010, 4,123 in 2011, 6,602 in 2012, and 6,424 in 2013. The number spiked in March 2012 surrounding the visit of Pope Benedict XVI to Cuba. It also spiked in December 2013 when there were at least 1,123 short-term detentions for political reasons. From January through April 2014, the number of short-term detentions for political reasons amounted to 3,821 detentions, far higher than the same period over the past several years.[15]

---

[11] Amnesty International, *Routine Repression, Political Short-Term Detentions and Harassment in Cuba,* March 2012.

[12] AI defines prisoners of conscience as those jailed because of their political, religious or other conscientiously-held beliefs, ethnic origin, sex, color, language, national or social origin, economic status, birth, sexual orientation or other status, provided they have neither used nor advocated violence.

[13] Information drawn from Amnesty International's webpage on Cuba at http://www.amnesty.org/en/region/cuba.

[14] Comisión Cubana de Derechos Humanos y Reconciliación Nacional (CCDHRN), "Lista Parcial de Sancionados o Procesados por Motivos Políticos en Cuba," 18 de Noviembre de 2013.

[15] CCDHRN, "Cuba: Algunos Actos de Represión Política en el Mes de Abril de 2014" 5 de mayo de 2014.

Ladies in White

A human rights group known as the Ladies in White (Las Damas de Blanco) was formed in April 2003 by the wives, mothers, daughters, sisters, and aunts of the members of the "group of 75" dissidents arrested a month earlier in Cuba's human rights crackdown. The group conducts peaceful protests calling for the unconditional release of political prisoners. Dressed in white, its members attend Mass each Sunday at St. Rita's Church in Havana and then walk along Fifth Avenue to a nearby park. The group has faced considerable government-orchestrated harassment and repression over the years, particularly when members have staged protest in other parts of Havana or other parts of the country. Both Amnesty International and the Department of State at various junctures have called for the end of harassment and attacks against the human rights group. A founding member and leader of the Ladies in White, Laura Pollán, died unexpectedly in a Havana hospital from respiratory complications on October 14, 2011.

On the weekend of February 18-19, 2012, Cuban Archbishop Dionisio Garcia reportedly helped evacuate 14 members of the Ladies in White who had sought refuge at the El Cobre Basilica in Santiago, Cuba, after the women received messages that they would face beatings by the police. In the lead up to the visit of Pope Benedict XVI to Cuba in March 2012, repression against the Ladies in White increased with numerous short-term detentions intended to block the human rights activists from attending planned activities.

Amnesty International issued an urgent action appeal in July 2012, calling on Cuban authorities to either charge three protestors—Ladies in White Niurka Luque Álvarez and Sonia Garro Alfonso, and Sonia's husband Ramón Alejandro Muñoz González—or release them. All three were first detained in March 2012 after the two women participated in a peaceful commemoration of the anniversary of Cuba's March 2003 human rights crackdown. Luque Álvarez ultimately was released in October 5, 2012, while both Garro Alfonso and her husband continue to be incarcerated.

With Cuba's new travel policy, current Ladies in White leader Berta Soler traveled abroad to Europe and the United States for almost three months beginning in March 2013. Soler traveled to several European countries, including Belgium to accept the European Parliament's Sakharov prize that the human rights group was awarded in 2005, and also visited Washington DC, and Miami. After her return to Cuba, Soler said that she would like to broaden the movement and establish delegations around the island to increase the group's membership. The group reportedly has a membership of around 300 nationwide.

Websites: http://www.damasdeblanco.com/, http://www.damasdeblanco.org

---

Internationally known Cuban democracy and human rights activist Oswaldo Payá was killed in a car accident in July 2012 in the eastern province of Granma along with another Cuban human rights activist Harold Cepero. Payá, whose death prompted expressions of sympathy from around the world, is probably best known for his work founding the Varela Project in 1996.[16] Two Europeans accompanying Payá were also in the crash: Jens Aron Modig, president of the Swedish Christian Democrats youth wing, who was a passenger; and Angel Carromero Barrios, a leader of the Spanish Popular Party's youth organization, who was driving. Carromero was convicted in October 2012 of vehicular manslaughter for speeding and sentenced to four years in prison; after diplomatic efforts by Spain, he was released in late December 2012 to serve the rest of his term in Spain. In early March 2013, however, Carromero maintained in an interview with the *Washington Post* that the car he was driving was struck from behind just before the accident and that he was heavily drugged when he admitted to driving recklessly.[17] Payá's daughter has called for the United Nations to conduct an independent investigation into the crash. Modig maintains that he was asleep at the time of the accident and does not remember any details.[18] In July 2012, the U.S. Senate approved S.Res. 525 (Nelson), calling for an impartial third-party investigation of the crash. The U.S. Department of State issued a statement on March 28, 2013, calling for an

---

[16] The project collected thousands of signatures supporting a national plebiscite for political reform in accordance with a provision of the Cuban Constitution.

[17] Peter Finn, "Account of Cuban Crash Adds to Mystery," *Washington Post*, March 6, 2013; "I Only Wish They Were Nightmares, and Not Memories," (Editorial, Opinion) *Washington Post*, March 6, 2013.

[18] "Cuba, Aron Medig Reitera en una Reunión con la Hija de Oswaldo Payá que No Recuerda Nada del Accidente," *European Press*, March 13, 2013.

independent international investigation into the circumstances leading to the death of Payá and Cepero.[19]

Over the past several years, numerous independent Cuban blogs have been established that are often critical of the Cuban government. The Cuban government has responded with its own team of official bloggers to counter and disparage the independent bloggers.[20] Cuban blogger Yoani Sánchez has received considerable international attention since late 2007 for her website, Generación Y, which includes commentary critical of the Cuban government. (Sánchez's website is available at http://generacionyen.wordpress.com/, and has links to numerous other independent newspaper 14ymedioCuban blogs and websites.) Sánchez has plans to launch an independent digital newspaper in Cuba, *14ymedio*, on May 21, 2014, which will be available on the Internet but distributed through a variety of methods in Cuba, including CDs, USB flash drives, and DVDs. In the 113th Congress, H.Res. 121 (Hastings, FL), introduced in March 2013, would honor Sánchez "for her ongoing efforts to challenge political, economic, and social repression by the Castro regime."

While the human rights situation in Cuba remains poor, the country has made some advances in recent years. In 2008, Cuba lifted a ban on Cubans staying in hotels that previously had been restricted to foreign tourists in a policy that had been pejoratively referred to as "tourist apartheid." In recent years, as the government has enacted limited economic reforms, it has been much more open to debate on economic issues. The Catholic Church, which played a prominent role in the release of political prisoners in 2010, has been active in broadening the debate on social and economic issues through its publications *Palabra Nueva* (New World) and *Espacio Laical* (Space for Laity).

In January 2013, Cuba took the significant step of eliminating its long-standing policy of requiring an exit permit and letter of invitation for Cubans to travel abroad (see "Cuba Alters Its Policy Regarding Exit Permits" below). The change has allowed prominent dissidents and human rights activists to travel abroad and return to Cuba. These have included blogger Yoani Sánchez; Berta Soler, leader of the Ladies in White; Rosa María Payá, the daughter of the late political dissident Oswaldo Payá; Antonio Rodiles of the "Estado de Sats" nongovernmental organization; Elizardo Sánchez of the CCDHRN; independent blogger Orlando Luis Pardo; and Jorge Luis García Pérez, known as Antúnez, who is the secretary general of the Orlando Zapata Tamayo National Front of Civic Resistance. Several dissidents, however, including those political prisoners who have been released on parole, have been restricted from traveling abroad. These have included human rights activists Dr. Oscar Biscet and José Daniel Ferrer.[21]

Prominent dissident economist Oscar Espinosa Chepe died in Spain on September 23, 2013, after battling chronic liver disease and cancer. Espinosa had been imprisoned in March 2003 as one of the "group of 75" dissidents, but was released on medical parole in November 2004. The Department of State issued a statement after Espinosa Chepe's death maintaining that "he was a tireless champion for improving economic policy and human rights in Cuba" and that "he remained optimistic that the country he loved would experience economic prosperity and democratic governance."[22] Espinosa Chepe traveled to Madrid in March 2013 for medical

---

[19] U.S. Department of State, Daily Press Briefing, March 28, 2013.

[20] Committee to Protect Journalists, "After the Black Spring, Cuba's New Repression," July 6, 2011.

[21] Fabiola Santiago, "Despite 'Reforms" Some Cubans Aren't Free to Travel," *Miami Herald*, March 12, 2013.

[22] U.S. Department of State, "Death of Cuban Economist and Activist Oscar Espinosa Chepe," Press Statement, (continued...)

treatment. He is survived by Miriam Leiva, a longtime human rights activist and independent journalist who helped found the Ladies in White.

Human Rights Reporting on Cuba

Amnesty International (AI), Human Rights in the Republic of Cuba, http://www.amnesty.org/en/region/cuba.

AI *Annual Report 2013*, section on Cuba, http://www.amnesty.org/en/region/cuba/report-2013.

AI, *"Routine Repression, Political Short-Term Detentions and Harassment in Cuba,"* March 2012, available at http://www.amnesty.org/en/library/asset/AMR25/007/2012/en/647943e7-b4eb-4d39-a5e3-ea061edb651c/amr2500720I2en.pdf.

Cuban Commission on Human Rights and National Reconciliation (Comisión Cubana de Derechos Humanos y Reconciliación Nacional, CCDHRN), the independent Havana-based human rights organization produces a monthly report on short-term detentions for political reasons.

CCDHRN, "Cuba: Algunos Actos de Represion Politica en el Mes de Abril," May 5, 2014, available at http://observacuba.org/wp-content/uploads/pdfs/2014/overview-abril2014.pdf.

Human Rights Watch (HRW), http://www.hrw.org/en/americas/cuba.

HRW's 2014 World Report maintains that "the Cuban government continues to repress individuals and groups who criticize the government or call for basic human rights," available at http://www.hrw.org/world-report/2014/country-chapters/cuba.

Inter-American Commission on Human Rights, Annual Report 2013, April 23, 2014, Chapter IV has a section on Cuba, available at: http://www.oas.org/en/iachr/docs/annual/2013/docs-en/AnnualReport-Chap4-Cuba.pdf.

U.S. Department of State, Country Report on Human Rights Practices for 2013, February 27, 2014, available at http://www.state.gov/documents/organization/220646.pdf. According to the report, Cuba's "principal human rights abuses were abridgement of the rights of citizens to change the government and the use of government threats, extrajudicial psychical violence, intimidation, mobs, harassment, and detentions to prevent free expression and peaceful assembly."

Economic Conditions and Reform Efforts

Cuba's economy is largely state-controlled, with the government owning most means of production and employing almost 80% of the workforce. Key sectors of the economy that generate foreign exchange include the export of professional services (largely medical personnel to Venezuela); tourism, which has grown significantly since the mid-1990s, with 2.8 million tourists visiting Cuba in 2012; nickel mining, with the Canadian mining company Sherritt International involved in a joint investment project; and a biotechnology and pharmaceutical sector that supplies the domestic healthcare system and has fostered a significant export industry. Remittances from relatives living abroad, especially from the United States, have also become an important source of hard currency, and are estimated to be between $1.4 billion and $2 billion annually. The once-dominant sugar industry has declined significantly over the past 20 years; in 1990, Cuba produced 8.4 million tons of sugar while in 2014 it produced just 1.6 million tons.[23]

(...continued)

September 23, 2013.

[23] Information and statistics were drawn from several sources: U.S. Department of State, "U.S. Relations with Cuba," August 30, 2013; Economist Intelligence Unit, "Cuba Country Report," February 2013; Oficina Nacional de Estadísticas, "Anuario Estadístico de Cuba, 2011"; and Marc Frank, "Cuban Sugar Out Tops Previous Harvest, But Well Below Plan," *Reuters*, May 19, 2014.

Cuba is highly dependent on Venezuela for its oil needs. In 2000, the two countries signed a preferential oil agreement that provides Cuba with some 100,000 barrels of oil per day, about two-thirds of its consumption. Cuba's goal of becoming a net oil exporter with the development of its offshore deepwater oil reserves was set back significantly in 2012 when three exploratory oil drills were unsuccessful. In another blow to Cuba's oil development in 2013, Russian energy company Zarubezhneft, which had been drilling an exploratory block in a coastal block in shallow waters, experienced problems with the oil rig and the geology of the area and stopped work on the drilling in April—the rig was redeployed to Asia in June. (For more, see "Cuba's Offshore Oil Development" below.)

The setback in Cuba's offshore oil development combined with recent political events in Venezuela (i.e., the death of President Chávez in March and a close presidential race in April) have raised concerns among Cuban officials about the security of the support received from Venezuela. Cuba is increasingly focusing on the need to diversify its trading partners and to seek alternative energy suppliers in the case of a cutback or cutoff of Venezuelan oil.[24]

Over the years, Cuba has expressed pride for the nation's accomplishments in health and education. According to the U.N. Development Program's 2013 Human Development Report, life expectancy in Cuba in 2012 was 79.3 years and adult literacy was estimated at almost 100%. The World Bank estimates that Cuba's per capita income level of $5,550 (2010, latest available) is in the upper-middle-income range, higher than a number of other countries in the Americas.[25]

In terms of economic growth, Cuba experienced severe economic deterioration from 1989 to 1993, with an estimated decline in gross domestic product ranging from 35% to 50% when the Soviet Union collapsed and Russian financial assistance to Cuba practically ended. Since then, however, there has been considerable improvement. From 1994 to 2000, as Cuba moved forward with some limited market-oriented economic reforms, economic growth averaged 3.7% annually. Economic growth was especially strong in the 2004-2007 period, registering an impressive 11% and 12%, respectively, in 2005 and 2006 (see **Figure 2**). The economy benefitted from the growth of the tourism, nickel, and oil sectors, and support from Venezuela and China in terms of investment commitments and credit lines. However, the economy was hard hit by several hurricanes and storms in 2008 and the global financial in 2009, with the government having to implement austerity measures. As a result, economic growth slowed significantly.

Since 2010, however, growth has improved modestly, with 2.4% growth in 2010, 2.8% in 2011, 3% in 2012, and 2.7% in 2013, according to the *Economist Intelligence Unit* (EIU). The forecast for 2014 is for 2.1% growth, but beyond that, the EIU maintains that Cuba's efforts to expand the private sector and boost productivity, along with favorable external conditions, could increase economic growth to an average of almost 4% in the 2015-2018 period, although a withdrawal of support from Venezuela would jeopardize these forecasts.[26] Some economists, however, maintain that Cuba needs a growth rate of at least 5% to 7% in order to develop the economy and create new jobs—increasing internal savings and attracting foreign investment reportedly are keys to achieving such growth rates.[27]

---

[24] For example, see "Cuba, Economy, Seeking New Partners, *Latin American Caribbean & Central America Report*, May 2013.

[25] World Bank, World Development Report 2012, p. 402.

[26] "Cuba Country Report," *Economist Intelligence Unit (EIU)*, April 2014.

[27] Marc Frank, "Factbox—Key Political Risks to Watch in Cuba," *Reuters News*, May 13, 2013.

Figure 2. Cuba: Real GDP Growth (percentage), 2004-2013

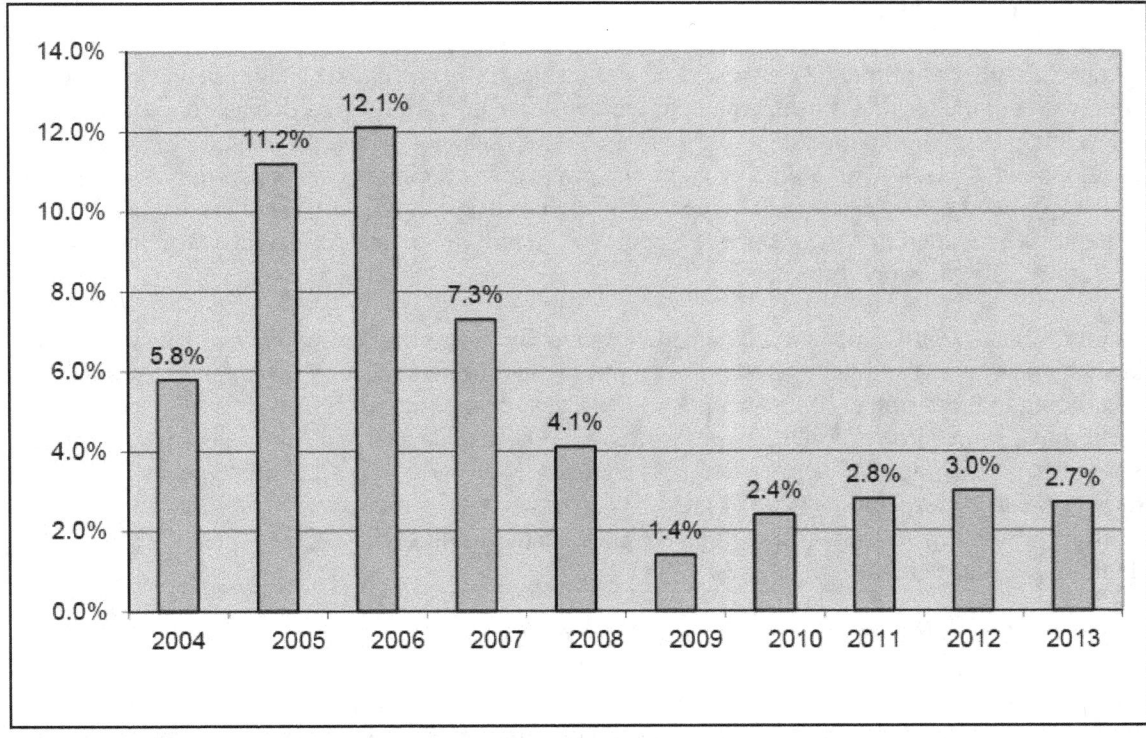

Source: Economist Intelligence Unit, Country Data Tool, 2014.

The government of Raúl Castro has implemented a number of economic policy changes, but there has been some disappointment that more far-reaching reforms have not been forthcoming. As noted above, the government employs a majority of the labor force, almost 80%, but it has been allowing more private sector activities. In 2010, the government opened up a wide range of activities for self-employment and small businesses. There are now almost 200 categories of work allowed, and the number of self-employed has risen from some 156,000 at the end of 2010 to some 440,000 today. [28] In 2013, some 125 non-agricultural cooperatives were established and the government announced that 20 state-run restaurants would be converted to cooperatives in a pilot project that could eventually lead to the conversion of hundreds of other state-run restaurants. [29]

Analysts contend, however, that the government needs to do more to support the development of the private sector, including an expansion of authorized activities to include more white-collar occupations and state support for credit to support small businesses. A major challenge for the development of the private sector is the lack of money in circulation. Most Cubans do not make enough money to support the development of small businesses; those private sector activities catering to tourists and foreign diplomats have fared better than those serving the Cuban market. The government's decisions in 2013 to crack down on privately run movie and video game salons and on private sales of imported clothes and hardware raised questions about its commitment to the development of the private sector. In late December 2013, Raúl Castro issued a warning

---

[28] Andrea Rodriguez and Anne Marie Garcia, "2 Years Into Cuba's Free Market Experiment, Small Entrepreneurs Struggle to Stay Afloat," *Associated Press*, December 27, 2013; Anne Marie Garcia, "Cuban Orders Immediate Ban on 3D, Other Movies, Video Games in Privately Run Businesses," *Associated Press*, November 2, 2013.

[29] Marc Frank, "Cuban State Begins to Move Out of the Restaurant Business," *Reuters News*, August 26, 2013.

against those engaging in economic activities not strictly authorized by the state, maintaining that it creates an environment of impunity.[30]

When the Cuban Communist Party held its sixth congress in April 2011, it approved over 300 economic guidelines that, if implemented, include some potentially significant economic reforms. These include the liquidation of state enterprises with financial losses, the creation of special development zones for foreign investment, the gradual development of a tax system as a means to distribute income, and a gradual elimination of the ration system.[31] Some economic analysts, however, maintained that the proposed changes were too limited and late to deal with the severity of Cuba's difficult economic situation.[32]

Among Cuba's significant economic challenges are low wages (whereby workers cannot satisfy basic human needs) and the related problem of how to unify Cuba's two official currencies circulating in the country.[33] Most people are paid in Cuban pesos (CUPs) and the minimum monthly wage in Cuba is about 225 pesos (about $9 U.S. dollars),[34] but for increasing amounts of consumer goods, convertible pesos (CUCs) are used. (For personal transactions, the exchange rate for the two currencies is CUP24/CUC1.) Cubans with access to foreign remittances or who work in jobs that give them access to convertible pesos are far better off than those Cubans who do not have such access.

In October 2013, the Cuban government announced that it would move toward ending its dual-currency system and move toward monetary unification. In early March 2014, the government provided insight about how monetary unification would move forward when it published instructions for when the CUC is removed from circulation; no date was provided, but it was referred to as day zero (*día cero*). The *Economist Intelligence Unit* believes that unification will happen before the end of 2014, but there is significant uncertainty about the actual date and the exchange rate system that will replace it.[35] The currency reform is ultimately expected to lead to productivity gains and improve the business climate, but the adjustment will create winners and losers.[36]

A significant reform effort under Raúl Castro has focused on the agricultural sector, a vital issue because Cuba reportedly imports some 60% of its food needs. In an effort to boost food

---

[30] Michael Weissenstein and Andrea Rodriguez, "Raúl Castro Issues Stern Warning to Entrepreneurs Pushing Boundaries of Cuba's Economic Reforms," *Associated Press*, December 21, 2013.

[31] *Lineamientos de la Política Económica y Social Del Partido y la Revolución*, VI Congreso del Partido Comunista de Cuba, approved April 18, 2011, available at http://thecubaneconomy.com/wp-content/uploads/2011/05/Lineamientos-de-la-Pol%C3%ADtica-econ%C3%B3mica-y-Social-del-Partido-y-la-Revoluci%C3%B3n-Aprobado-el-18-de-abril-de-2011.-VI-Congreso-del-PCC.pdf. In addition, the Cuban Communist Party published a report comparing the original 291 guidelines to the final 313 guidelines and how they changed. See *Información Sobre el Resultado del Debate de los Lineamientos de la Política Económica y Social Del Partido y la Revolución*, VI Congreso del Partido Comunista de Cuba, May 2011, available at http://www.cubadebate.cu/wp-content/uploads/2011/05/tabloide_debate_lineamientos.pdf.

[32] Oscar Espinosa Chepe, *Cambios en Cuba: Pocos, Limitados y Tardios*, Havana Cuba, February 2011, available at http://reconciliacioncubana.files.wordpress.com/2011/03/cambios-en-cuba.pdf.

[33] For more on Cuba's currency problem, see "Replacing Cuba's Dual Currency System: What Are the Issues that Really Matter?," *Latin American Economy & Business*, July 2013.

[34] U.S. Department of State, "Country Reports on Human Rights Practices for 2013, Cuba," February 27, 2014.

[35] "Cuba Country Report," *EIU*, April 2014.

[36] "Cuba: Exchange Rate Unification Approaching," *Latin America Regional Report: Caribbean & Central America*, March 2014.

---

production, the government has turned over idle land to farmers and given farmers more control over how to use their land and what supplies to buy. Despite these and other efforts, overall food production has been significantly below targets. In 2012, Cuba's coffee sector was hard hit by Hurricane Sandy in October, and overall agricultural production reportedly underperformed for the year. In November 2013, the Cuban government unveiled a new pilot program for the provinces of Havana, Artemisa, and Mayabeque that will end the government's monopoly on food distribution in an effort to boost production.[37]

In late March 2014, Cuba approved a new foreign investment law (to go into effect in 90 days) with the goal of attracting needed foreign capital to the country. The law cuts taxes in profits by half to 15% and exempts companies from paying taxes for the first eight years of operation. Employment or labor taxes are also eliminated, although companies still must hire labor through state-run companies, with agreed upon wages. A fast-track procedure for small projects reportedly will streamline the approval process, and the government has agreed to improve the transparency and time of the approval process for larger investments.[38] It remains to be seen, however, to what extent the new law will actually attract investment. Over the past several years, Cuba has closed a number of joint ventures with foreign companies and has arrested several executives of foreign companies reportedly for corrupt practices. According to some observers, investors will want evidence, not just legislation, that the government is prepared to allow foreign investors to make a profit in Cuba.[39]

In late April 2014, the Cuban government loosened restrictions on hundreds of its largest state-run companies that reportedly will be allowed to keep 50% of their profits after taxes, design their own wage systems, sell excess product on the open market after meeting state quotas, and have more flexibility in production and marketing decisions.[40]

For Additional Reading on the Cuban Economy

Association for the Study of the Cuban Economy, Annual Proceedings, available at http://www.ascecuba.org/publications/proceedings/.

Brookings Institution, webpage on Cuba, http://www.brookings.edu/research/topics/cuba;

Philip Peters, "Cuba's New Real Estate Market," February 2014, available at http://www.brookings.edu/~/media/research/files/reports/2014/02/21%20cuba%20real%20estate/phil%20peters%20cubas%20new%20real%20estate%20market.pdf; and

Richard Feinberg, "Soft Landing in Cuba? Emerging Entrepreneurs and Middle Classes," November 2013, available at http://www.brookings.edu/research/reports/2013/11/cuba-entrepreneurs-middle-classes-feinberg.

The Cuban Economy, La Economia Cubana, website maintained by Arch Ritter, from Carlton University, Ottawa, Canada, available at http://thecubaneconomy.com/.

Revista Temas (Havana), links to the Cuban journal's articles on Economy and Politics, in Spanish available at

---

[37] Marc Frank, "Cuba Growing Less Food than 5 Ys Ago Despite Agriculture Reforms," *Reuters*, August 31, 2012, "Cuba Sees Economy Growing 3.1 Pct in 2012, Below Forecast," *Reuters*, December 3, 2012, "Cuba Reports Little Progress Five Years into Agricultural Reform," *Reuters*, July 30, 2013, and "Cuba Rolls Out Master Plan for Food Production and Distribution," *Reuters News*, November 8, 2013.

[38] "Cuba Approves New Foreign Investment Law," *Latin American Regional Report: Caribbean & Central America*, April 2014; "What's Changed in Cuba's New Foreign Investment Law," *Reuters News*, March 29, 2014.

[39] Marc Frank, "Cuba Plans Big Tax Breaks to Lure Foreign Investors," Reuters News, March 26, 2014; and Daniel Trotta, "Cuba's Past Raises Skepticism About New Foreign Investment Law," *Reuters News*, March 31, 2014.

[40] Marc Frank, "Cuba's Market Reforms Spread to Largest Companies," *Reuters News*, April 28, 2014.

http://www.temas.cult.cu/catalejo.php.

Oficina Nacional de Estadísticas, República de Cuba, (Cuba's official economic statistics) available at http://www.one.cu/.

Cuba's Foreign Relations

During the Cold War, Cuba had extensive relations with and support from the Soviet Union, with billions of dollars in annual subsidies to sustain the Cuban economy. This subsidy system helped fund an activist foreign policy and support for guerrilla movements and revolutionary governments abroad in Latin America and Africa. With an end to the Cold War, the dissolution of the Soviet Union, and the loss of Soviet financial support, Cuba was forced to abandon its revolutionary activities abroad.

As its economy reeled from the loss of Soviet support, Cuba was forced to open up its economy and economic relations with countries worldwide, and it developed significant trade and investment linkages with Canada, Spain, other European countries, and China. Over the past decade, Venezuela—under populist President Hugo Chávez—became a significant source of support for Cuba, providing subsidized oil (some 100,000 barrels per day) and investment. For its part, Cuba has sent thousands of medical personnel to Venezuela. In the aftermath of Chávez's death in early March 2013 and the very close presidential election in April 2013 won by Nicolás Maduro of the ruling Socialist party by just 1.49% over the opposition candidate, Henrique Capriles, Cuban officials are concerned about the future of Venezuelan support in the medium to longer term. During the Venezuelan election campaign, Capriles had vowed to end the shipment of subsidized oil to Cuba.

In 2012, Cuba's leading trading partners in terms of Cuban exports were Venezuela, the Netherlands, Canada, and China (see **Figure 3**), while the leading sources of Cuba's imports were Venezuela, China, Spain, Brazil, and the United States (see **Figure 4**).

Relations with Russia, which had diminished significantly in the aftermath of the Cold War, were strengthened with the November 2008 visit of then-Russian President Dmitry Medvedev to Havana, the visit of several Russian warships to Cuba in December 2008, and Raúl Castro's visit to Russia in January 2009. Castro visited Russia again in July 2012, with the goal reportedly to increase and diversify trade and investment. While trade relations between the two countries are not significant, two Russian energy companies have been involved in oil exploration in Cuba. Gazprom has been in a partnership with the Malaysian state oil company Petronas that conducted unsuccessful deepwater oil drilling off of Cuba's western coast in 2012. The Russian oil company Zarubezhneft began drilling in Cuba's shallow coastal waters east of Havana in December 2012, but stopped work in April 2013 because of disappointing results (also see "Cuba's Offshore Oil Development" below). In February 2013, Russian Prime Minister Medvedev visited Cuba and signed 10 bilateral accords, including an accord that reportedly would lead to an agreement to write off the majority of Soviet era debt owed by Cuba.[41] The two countries followed up in December 2013 with an agreement writing off 90% of Cuba's $32 billion debt owed to the Soviet Union, with Cuba agreeing to pay $3.2 billion to Russia over a t10-year period.[42]

---

[41] "Castro Declares He Had 'a Good Visit" with Russia's Medvedev," *Agence France Presse*, February 23, 2013.

[42] Marc Frank, "Russia Signs Deal to Forgive $29 Bln of Cuba's Soviet-Era Debt – Diplomats," *Reuters*, December 9, (continued...)

Figure 3. Cuban Exports by Country of Destination, 2012

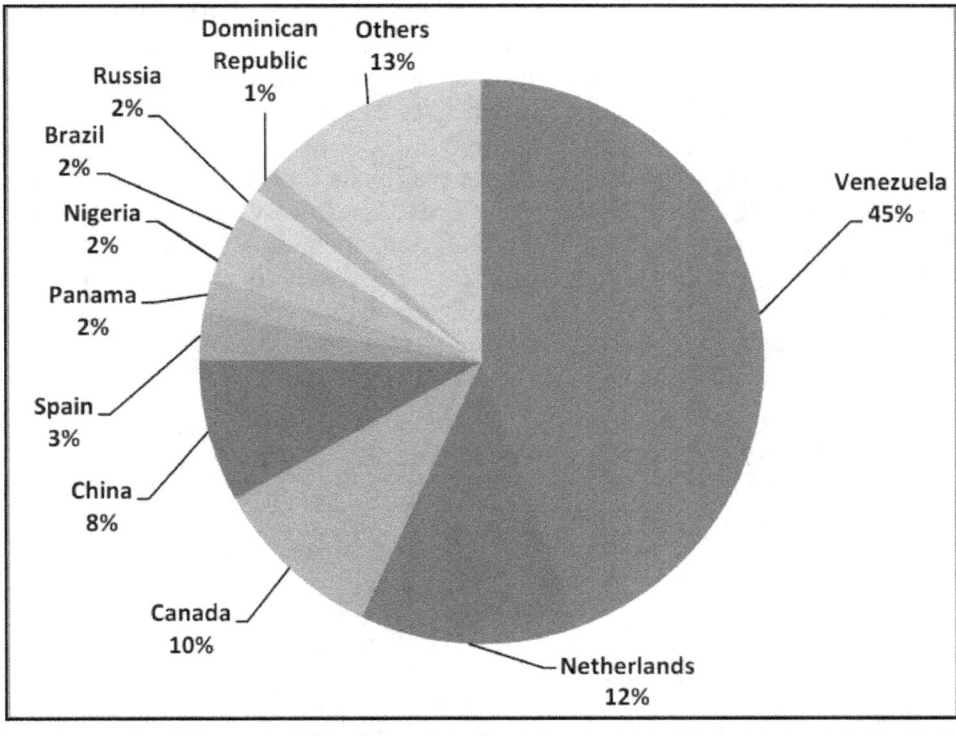

Source: Created by CRS based on information from República de Cuba, Oficina Nacional de Estadística e Informacíon, Anuario Estadístico de Cuba 2012, Sector Externo, Table 8.5, http://www.one.cu/aec2012/esp/ 20080618_tabla_cuadro.htm.

Relations with China have also increased in recent years. Chinese President Hu Jintao visited Cuba in November 2008, signing a dozen agreements, while Chinese Vice President Xi Jinping visited Cuba in June 2011. During the Xi Jinping visit, China signed a letter of intent to invest in upgrading a Cuban oil refinery in Cienfuegos. In July 2012, President Castro visited China on a four-day visit; the two countries reportedly signed eight cooperation agreements with talks focusing on trade and investment issues. (After China, Castro visited Vietnam on a four-day trip. The two countries have long had good relations, and some observers speculate that Cuba looks to Vietnam for potential lessons in implementing economic reforms.)

With El Salvador's restoration of relations with Cuba in June 2009, all Latin American nations now have official diplomatic relations with Cuba. Cuba has increasingly become more engaged in Latin America beyond the already close relations with Venezuela. Cuba is a member of the Bolivarian Alliance for the Americas, (ALBA), a Venezuelan-led integration and cooperation scheme founded in 2004. In August 2013, Cuba began deploying thousands of doctors to Brazil in a program aimed at providing doctors to rural areas of Brazil, with Cuba earning some $225 million a year for supplying the medical personnel.[43] Brazil also has been a major investor in the development of the port of Mariel west of Havana.

(...continued)

2013.

[43] Anthony Boadle, "Cuban Doctors Tend to Brazil's Poor, Giving Rousseff a Boost," *Reuters News*, December 1, 2013.

Cuba became a full member of the Rio Group of Latin American and Caribbean nations in November 2008, and a member of the succeeding Community of Latin American and Caribbean States (CELAC) that was officially established in December 2011 to boost regional cooperation, but without the participation of the United States or Canada. In January 2013, CELAC held its first summit in Chile, and Raúl Castro assumed the presidency of the organization for one year. Cuba hosted the group's second summit on January 28-29, 2014 in Havana, attended by leaders from across the hemisphere as well as U.N. Secretary General Ban Ki-moon and OAS Secretary General José Miguel Insulza. The U.N. Secretary General reportedly raised human rights issues with Cuban officials, including the subject of Cuba's ratification of U.N. human rights accords and "arbitrary detentions" by the Cuban government.[44] Dozens of dissidents were arrested or detained in the lead-up to the summit. At the summit, Latin American nations approved a joint declaration emphasizing nonintervention and pledging to respect "the inalienable right of every state to choose its political, economic, social and cultural system."[45]

Figure 4. Cuban Imports by Country of Origin, 2012

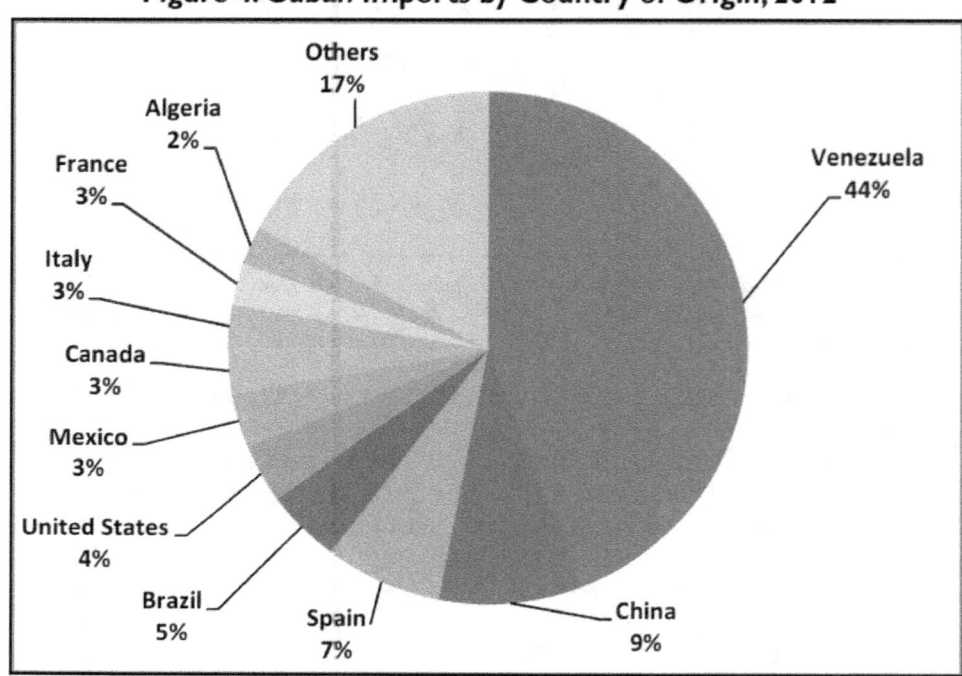

Source: Created by CRS based on information from República de Cuba, Oficina Nacional de Estadística e Informacíon, Anuario Estadístico de Cuba 2012, Sector Externo, Table 8.6, http://www.one.cu/aec2012/esp/20080618_tabla_cuadro.htm.

Cuba had expressed interest in attending the sixth Summit of the Americas in April 2012 in Cartagena, Colombia, but ultimately was not invited to attend. The United States and Canada expressed opposition to Cuba's participation. Previous summits have been limited to the hemisphere's 34 democratically elected leaders, and the OAS (in which Cuba does not participate) has played a key role in summit implementation and follow-up activities. Several Latin American nations, however, have vowed not to attend the next Summit of the Americas to be held in Panama in 2015 unless Cuba is allowed to participate.

---

[44] "UN Chief Pushes Cuba on 'Arbitrary Detentions,'" *Agence France Presse*, January 28, 2014.

[45] Peter Orsi, "LatAm Leaders Declare Region a 'Zone of Peace,'" *Associated Press*, January 29, 2014.

Cuba was excluded from participation in the OAS in 1962 because of its identification with Marxism-Leninism, but in early June 2009, the OAS overturned the 1962 resolution in a move that could eventually lead to Cuba's reentry into the regional organization in accordance with the practices, purposes, and principles of the OAS. While the Cuban government welcomed the OAS vote to overturn the 1962 resolution, it asserted that it would not return to the OAS.[46]

Cuba is an active participant in international forums, including the United Nations and the controversial United Nations Human Rights Council. Since 1991, the U.N. General Assembly has approved a resolution each year criticizing the U.S. economic embargo and urging the United States to lift it. Cuba also has received support over the years from the United Nations Development Programme (UNDP) and the United Nations Educational, Scientific, and Cultural Organization (UNESCO), both of which have offices in Havana. The U.N. has played a significant role in providing relief and recovery from Hurricane Sandy that struck in October 2012. In November 2012, the U.N. system launched a Plan of Action (developed in cooperation with the Cuban government) for $30.6 million to address the urgent needs of the population in the following sectors: shelter and recovery, water sanitation and hygiene, food security, health, and education.[47]

Among other international organizations, Cuba was a founding member of the World Trade Organization, but it is not a member of the International Monetary Fund, the World Bank, or the Inter-American Development Bank. Cuba hosted the 14th summit of the Non-aligned Movement (NAM) in 2006, and held the Secretary Generalship of the NAM until its July 2009 summit in Egypt.

North Korean Ship Incident[48]

On July 10, 2013, Panamanian authorities detained a North Korean freighter known as the *Chong Chon Gang*, which made stops in Cuba, as it prepared to enter the Panama Canal because of suspicion that the ship was carrying illicit narcotics. The ship, which had stops Cuba at Havana and Puerto Padre (a major sugar export point), was taken to Panama's international container port of Manzanillo in Panama's Colón province. When Panamanian authorities attempted to detain and search the ship, the 35-member North Korean crew tried to prevent them, and the captain attempted to commit suicide.[49] Panama's initial search of the ship found weapons hidden aboard along with sugar. Panama's President Ricardo Martinelli made a public radio broadcast to that effect on July 15 and also tweeted a photo of some of the military equipment found.

---

[46] For further background, see section on "Cuba and the OAS" in archived CRS Report R40193, *Cuba: Issues for the 111th Congress*, by Mark P. Sullivan; also see CRS Report R42639, *Organization of American States: Background and Issues for Congress*, by Peter J. Meyer.

[47] U.N. OCHA, "Cuba, Plan of Action, Response to Needs Arising from Hurricane Sandy," November 2012, available at http://reliefweb.int/sites/reliefweb.int/files/resources/CUBA%20Action%20Plan%20FINAL.pdf.

[48] Also see September 26, 2013 CRS testimony to Congress presented by Mary Beth Nikitin, Specialist in Nonproliferation, before the House Committee on Foreign Affairs, Subcommittee on the Western Hemisphere, at a hearing entitled "A Closer Look at Cuba and Its Recent History of Proliferation," available at http://docs.house.gov/meetings/FA/FA07/20130926/101353/HHRG-113-FA07-Wstate-NikitinM-20130926.pdf. Other hearing testimony is available at http://foreignaffairs.house.gov/hearing/subcommittee-hearing-closer-look-cuba-and-its-recent-history-proliferation.

[49] Rick Gladstone and David E. Sanger, "Panama Seizes Korean Ship, And Sugar-Coated Arms Parts," *New York Times*, July 17, 2013.

Cuba's Ministry of Foreign Affairs subsequently issued a statement on July 16 acknowledging that the ship was loaded with 10,000 tons of sugar and 240 metric tons of "obsolete defensive weapons" that had been manufactured in the mid-20th century and were to be "repaired and returned to Cuba" in order to maintain the country's defensive capability. Cuba maintained that the weapons being transported on the ship were "two anti-aircraft missiles complexes Volga and Pechora, nine missiles in parts and spares, two MiG-21 Bis and 15 motors for this type of airplane."[50]

Cuba's statement raised questions as to why Cuba would make such an effort to repair what it described as "obsolete defensive equipment." Some press reports indicated that Cuba was attempting to have the missile systems upgraded by North Korea. Jeffrey Lewis from the Monterey Institute for International Studies maintains that the explanation that North Korea was refurbishing Cuba's anti-aircraft missiles was plausible since it clears up a mystery as to how Cuba had been able to introduced new missile launchers in 2006 for two types of missiles.[51] The sugar could have been Cuba's payment—essentially a barter arrangement for the repair/upgrade of the weapons. For some analysts, however, the inclusion of the MiGs in the shipment raises skepticism as to whether the MiGs and engines were going to be returned to Cuba. In 2011, North Korea had attempted to acquire parts of MiG-21 jets from Mongolia, according to a June 2013 report by the U.N. Security Council's Panel of Experts.[52]

In late August, the Stockholm International Peace Research Institute (SPRI) issued a report maintaining that key parts of Cuba's military shipment to North Korea "seem intended for Pyongyang's own use in its conventional military defenses, not to be repaired and returned to Cuba." In addition to the materiel that Cuba publicly acknowledged, the SPPRI report maintained that the North Korean "ship also was transporting a variety of small arms and light weapons (SALW) ammunition and conventional artillery ammunition for anti-tank guns and howitzer artillery as well as generators, batteries, and night vision equipment, among other items." Some of this materiel was reported to be in "mint condition" and "clearly were not to be repaired and returned to Cuba."[53]

The discovery of the *Chong Chon Gang* shipment of weapons also raises questions about the potential previous shipment of weapons from Cuba to North Korea and more broadly about the nature of Cuban-North Korean relations. According to press reports, North Korean ships have made several other trips to Cuba since 2009.[54] The Wisconsin Project on Nuclear Arms Control reports that two North Korean vessels, the *O Un Chong Nyon Ho* and the *Mu Du Bong*, traveled to Cuba in May 2012 and May 2009 respectively.[55] In particular, the *O Un Chong Nyon Ho* was

---

[50] Cuba, Ministry of Foreign Affairs, "Statement by the Ministry of Foreign Affairs," July 16, 2013.

[51] Jeffrey Lewis, "Chen Chon Gang Interdiction," Arms Control Wonk, Leading Blogs on Arms Control, Disarmament and Non-proliferation, July 18, 2013, available at http://lewis.armscontrolwonk.com/archive/6705/chong-chon-gang-interdiction.

[52] U.N. Security Council, Panel of Experts Pursuant to Resolution 1874 (2009), Report S/2013/337, June 13, 2013, available at http://www.un.org/ga/search/view_doc.asp?symbol=S/2013/337.

[53] Hugh Griffiths and Roope Siirtola, "Full Disclosure: Contents of North Korean Smuggling Ship Revealed," Stockholm International Peace Research Institute, published online by 38 North, a project of the U.S. Korean Institute at Johns Hopkins School of Advanced International Studies, available at http://38north.org/2013/08/hgriffiths082713/.

[54] Billy Kenber, "Soviet-Era Weaponry Found Hidden on North Korean Freighter," *Washington Post*, July 21, 2013; and Juan O. Tamayo, "Al Menos Cinco Cargueros Norcoreanos Han Visitado Cuba Desde el 2009," *El Nuevo Herald*, July 25, 2013.

[55] "More on the North Korean Vessel Seized in Panama," Wisconsin Project on Nuclear Arms Control, July 17, 2013, (continued...)

---

reported to have visited the same two Cuban ports as the *Chong Chon Gang* – Havana and the sugar export center of Puerto Padre. Another North Korean ship, the *Po Thong Gang*, also reportedly docked at Puerto Padre in April 2012, and at the ports of Havana and Santiago de Cuba in 2011.[56]

Relations between Cuba and North Korea traditionally have not been thought to be significant. During the Cold War, North Korea was an ideological partner of Cuba since both countries sided with the Soviet Union, but the relationship was not thought to go beyond political and ideological relations. Former Cuban President Fidel Castro acknowledged that North Korea had provided 100,000 Kalashnikov assault weapons to Cuba in the early 1980s.[57] While North Korea has a history of buying and selling arms around the world, it was not thought to have a significant arms trade relationship with Cuba.[58] Nevertheless, the recent visit of a high-level North Korean military delegation to Cuba in early July 2013, less than 10 days before the detention of the *Chong Chon Gang*, might provide some insight into the bilateral military relationship between the two countries. The North Korean delegation, led by General Kim Kyok Sik, Chief of the Korean People's Army General Staff, met with Cuban President Raúl Castro, who stressed the historic ties between the two countries and efforts to boost cooperative relations.[59]

Panama asked the U.N. Security Council to investigate the shipment and determine whether Cuba violated U.N. sanctions banning weapons transfers to North Korea.[60] In response, the U.N. Panel of Experts for North Korea visited Panama August 13-15, 2013. In late August 2013, Panamanian officials maintain that they were given a preliminary version that reportedly concluded that the Cuban weapons found on the *Chong Chon Gang* "without doubt" violated U.N. sanctions.[61]

In early March 2014, the U.N. Security Council issued the Panel of Experts report, which stated that the panel had concluded in its incident report that both the shipment itself and the transaction between Cuba and North Korea were sanctions violations. The panel found that the "hidden cargo ... amounted to six trailers associated with surface-to-air missile systems and 25 shipping containers loaded with two disassembled MiG-21 aircraft, 15 engines for MiG-21 aircraft, components for surface to air missile systems, ammunition and miscellaneous arms-related material." The panel found that the "extraordinary and extensive efforts to conceal the cargo of arms and related material ... and the contingency instructions ... found onboard the vessel for preparing a false declaration for entering the Panama Canal ... point to a clear and conscious intention to circumvent the resolutions."[62]

(...continued)

available at http://www.wisconsinproject.org/pubs/editorials/chongchongang.htm.

[56] Kenber, op. cit. and Tamayo, op. cit.

[57] "Castro Says N.K. Supplied Free Weapons to Cuba," *The Korea Herald*, August 16, 2013; and Peter Orsi, "Cuba's Fidel Castro Says He Never Imagined He'd Live to 87 When Serious Illness Struck in 2006," *AP Newswire*, August 14, 2013.

[58] Foster Klug, "A Look at North Korea's Long History of Buying, Marketing and Selling Arms Around the World," *Associated Press*, July 17, 2013.

[59] "North Korea Military Delegation Holds Talks With Cuban Leader," *BBC Monitoring Asia Pacific*, July 2, 2013.

[60] U.N. Security Council sanctions ban all weapons exports from North Korea, and all imports except small arms and light weapons.

[61] Lomi Kriel, "Panama Says Cuban Weapons Shipment 'Without Doubt' Violated UN Sanctions," *Reuters*, August 28, 2013.

[62] United Nations Security Council, Notes by the President of the Security Council, Report of the Panel of Experts (continued...)

U.S. Policy Toward Cuba

Background on U.S.-Cuban Relations[63]

In the early 1960s, U.S.-Cuban relations deteriorated sharply when Fidel Castro began to build a repressive communist dictatorship and moved his country toward close relations with the Soviet Union. The often tense and hostile nature of the U.S.-Cuban relationship is illustrated by such events and actions as U.S. covert operations to overthrow the Castro government culminating in the ill-fated April 1961 Bay of Pigs invasion; the October 1962 missile crisis in which the United States confronted the Soviet Union over its attempt to place offensive nuclear missiles in Cuba; Cuban support for guerrilla insurgencies and military support for revolutionary governments in Africa and the Western Hemisphere; the 1980 exodus of around 125,000 Cubans to the United States in the so-called Mariel boatlift; the 1994 exodus of more than 30,000 Cubans who were interdicted and housed at U.S. facilities in Guantanamo and Panama; and the February 1996 shootdown by Cuban fighter jets of two U.S. civilian planes operated by the Cuban American group Brothers to the Rescue, which resulted in the death of four U.S. crew members.

Since the early 1960s, U.S. policy toward Cuba has consisted largely of isolating the island nation through comprehensive economic sanctions, including an embargo on trade and financial transactions. The Cuban Assets Control Regulations (CACR), first issued by the Treasury Department in July 1963, lay out a comprehensive set of economic sanctions against Cuba, including a prohibition on most financial transactions with Cuba and a freeze of Cuban government assets in the United States. The CACR have been amended many times over the years to reflect changes in policy, and remain in force today.

These sanctions were made stronger with the Cuban Democracy Act (CDA) of 1992 (P.L. 102-484, Title XVII) and with the Cuban Liberty and Democratic Solidarity Act of 1996 (P.L. 104-114), the latter often referred to as the Helms/Burton legislation. The CDA prohibits U.S. subsidiaries from engaging in trade with Cuba and prohibits entry into the United States for any sea-borne vessel to load or unload freight if it has been involved in trade with Cuba within the previous 180 days. The Cuban Liberty and Democratic Solidarity Act, enacted in the aftermath of Cuba's shooting down of two U.S. civilian planes in February 1996, combines a variety of measures to increase pressure on Cuba and provides for a plan to assist Cuba once it begins the transition to democracy. Most significantly, the law codified the Cuban embargo, including all restrictions under the CACR. This provision is noteworthy because of its long-lasting effect on U.S. policy options toward Cuba. The executive branch is circumscribed in lifting the economic embargo without congressional concurrence until certain democratic conditions are met, although the CACR includes licensing authority that provides the executive branch with administrative flexibility (e.g., travel-related restrictions in the CACR have been eased and tightened on numerous occasions). Another significant sanction in the law is a provision in Title III that holds any person or government that traffics in U.S. property confiscated by the Cuban government

---

(...continued)

established pursuant to resolution 1874 (2009), S/1014/147, March 6, 2014, available at http://www.un.org/en/ga/search/view_doc.asp?symbol=S/2014/147.

[63] For additional background, see archived CRS Report RL30386, *Cuba-U.S. Relations: Chronology of Key Events 1959-1999*, by Mark P. Sullivan.

liable for monetary damages in U.S. federal court. Acting under provisions of the law, however, Presidents Clinton, Bush, and now Obama have suspended the implementation of Title III at six-month intervals.

In addition to sanctions, another component of U.S. policy, a so-called second track, consists of support measures for the Cuban people. This includes U.S. private humanitarian donations, medical exports to Cuba under the terms of the Cuban Democracy Act of 1992, U.S. government support for democracy-building efforts, and U.S.-sponsored radio and television broadcasting to Cuba. In addition, the 106th Congress approved the Trade Sanctions Reform and Export Enhancement Act of 2000 (P.L. 106-387, Title IX) that allows for agricultural exports to Cuba, albeit with restrictions on financing such exports. This led to the United States becoming one of Cuba's largest suppliers of agricultural products.

Clinton Administration's Easing of Sanctions

The Clinton Administration made several changes to U.S. policy in the aftermath of Pope John Paul II's 1998 visit to Cuba, which were intended to bolster U.S. support for the Cuban people. These included the resumption of direct flights to Cuba (which had been curtailed after the February 1996 shootdown of two U.S. civilian planes), the resumption of cash remittances by U.S. nationals and residents for the support of close relatives in Cuba (which had been curtailed in August 1994 in response to the migration crisis with Cuba), and the streamlining of procedures for the commercial sale of medicines and medical supplies and equipment to Cuba.

In January 1999, President Clinton announced several additional measures to support the Cuban people. These included a broadening of cash remittances to Cuba, so that all U.S. residents (not just those with close relatives in Cuba) could send remittances to Cuba; an expansion of direct passenger charter flights to Cuba from additional U.S. cities other than Miami (direct flights later in the year began from Los Angeles and New York); and an expansion of people-to-people contact by loosening restrictions on travel to Cuba for certain categories of travelers, such as professional researchers and those involved in a wide range of educational, religious, and sports activities.

Bush Administration's Tightening of Sanctions

The George W. Bush Administration essentially continued the two-track U.S. policy of isolating Cuba through economic sanctions while supporting the Cuban people through a variety of measures. However, within this policy framework, the Administration emphasized stronger enforcement of economic sanctions and further tightened restrictions on travel, remittances, and humanitarian gift parcels to Cuba. The Administration established an interagency Commission for Assistance to a Free Cuba in late 2003 tasked with identifying means "to help the Cuban people bring about an expeditious end of the dictatorship" and to consider "the requirements for United States assistance to a post-dictatorship Cuba."[64] In issuing its first report in May 2004, the commission made recommendations to tighten restrictions on family visits and other categories of travel and on private humanitarian assistance in the form of remittances and gift parcels.[65] The Administration subsequently issued these tightened restrictions in June 2004, while in February

---

[64] U.S. Department of State, "Commission for Assistance to a Free Cuba," White House Fact Sheet, December 8, 2003.

[65] See the commission's May 2004 report, available at http://pdf.usaid.gov/pdf_docs/PCAAB192.pdf.

2005, it tightened restrictions on payment terms for U.S. agricultural exports to Cuba. The commission issued a second and final report in July 2006 that made recommendations to hasten political change in Cuba toward a democratic transition and led to a substantial increase in U.S. funding to support democracy and human rights efforts in Cuba.

The Bush Administration continued to emphasize a continuation of the sanctions-based approach toward Cuba pending political change in Cuba. When Raúl Castro officially became head of state in February 2008, then-Secretary of State Condoleezza Rice issued a statement urging "the Cuban government to begin a process of peaceful, democratic change by releasing all political prisoners, respecting human rights, and creating a clear pathway towards free and fair elections."[66] In remarks on Cuba policy in March 2008, President Bush maintained that in order to improve U.S.-Cuban relations, "what needs to change is not the United States; what needs to change is Cuba." The President asserted that Cuba "must release all political prisoners ... have respect for human rights in word and deed, and pave the way for free and fair elections."[67]

Obama Administration Policy

In some respects, the Obama Administration has continued the dual-track policy approach toward Cuba that has been in place for many years. It has largely maintained U.S. economic sanctions and it has continued measures to support the Cuban people, such as U.S. government-sponsored radio and television broadcasting and funding for democracy and human rights projects.

At the same time, a significant shift in policy toward Cuba under the Obama Administration has occurred with its efforts to reach out to the Cuban people through the easing of restrictions on travel and remittances. In April 2009, the Obama Administration fulfilled a campaign pledge and announced it would lift all restrictions on family travel and remittances. The Administration went further in January 2011 when it announced new measures to ease travel restrictions and to allow all Americans to send remittances to Cuba. The measures increased purposeful travel to Cuba related to religious, educational, and journalistic activities, including people-to-people travel exchanges; authorized any U.S. person to send remittances to non-family members in Cuba; made it easier for religious institutions to send remittances for religious activities; and allowed all U.S. international airports to apply to provide flights to and from Cuba.

In 2012 congressional testimony, Assistant Secretary of State for Western Hemisphere Affairs Roberta Jacobson asserted that "the Obama Administration's priority is to empower Cubans to freely determine their own future." She maintained that "the most effective tool we have for doing that is building connections between the Cuban and American people, in order to give Cubans the support and tools they need to move forward independent of their government." The Assistant Secretary maintained that "the Administration's travel, remittance and people-to-people policies are helping Cubans by providing alternative sources of information, taking advantage of emerging opportunities for self-employment and private property, and strengthening civil society."[68]

---

[66] U.S. Department of State, Secretary of State Condoleezza Rice, "Statement on Cuba's Transition," February 24, 2008.

[67] White House, "President Bush Delivers Remarks on Cuba," March 7, 2008.

[68] U.S. Department of State, "The Path to Freedom Countering Repression and Strengthening Civil Society in Cuba," Testimony by Roberta S. Jacobson, Assistant Secretary, Bureau of Western Hemisphere Affairs, Senate Foreign Relations Committee, Subcommittee on the Western Hemisphere, June 7, 2012, available at http://www.state.gov/p/ (continued...)

When the Obama Administration took office in 2009, it initiated a policy to engage with the Cuban government in an effort to improve relations. At the April 2009 Summit of the Americas, President Obama announced that "the United States seeks a new beginning with Cuba." While recognizing that it would take time to "overcome decades of mistrust," the President said "there are critical steps we can take toward a new day." He stated that he was prepared to have his Administration "engage with the Cuban government on a wide range of issues—from drugs, migration, and economic issues, to human rights, free speech, and democratic reform." The President maintained that he was "not interested in talking just for the sake of talking," but said that he believed that U.S.-Cuban relations could move in a new direction.[69] In the aftermath of the Summit, there appeared to be some momentum toward improved relations. In July 2009, Cuba and the United States restarted the semi-annual migration talks that had been suspended by the United States five years earlier. In September 2009, the United States and Cuba held talks in Havana on resuming direct mail service between the two countries that included discussion on issues related to the transportation, quality, and security of mail service.

Relations took a turn for the worse in December 2009, however, when Alan Gross, an American subcontractor working on Cuba democracy projects funded by the U.S. Agency for International Development (USAID) was arrested in Havana state for providing Internet communications equipment to Cuba's Jewish community. Gross was convicted in March 2011, and sentenced to 15 years in prison. U.S. officials and Members of Congress repeatedly have raised the issue with the Cuban government and asked for his release. In the aftermath of Gross's conviction, the United States and Cuba continued to cooperate on such issues as antidrug efforts and oil spill prevention, preparedness, and response, but improvement of relations in other areas appeared to have been stymied because of the Gross case.

Since June 2013, there has been renewed engagement with Cuba on several fronts, including direct mail service talks, resumed migration talks, and a preliminary agreement on air and maritime search and rescue.

- Talks for direct mail service between the United States on Cuba were held in June 2013 in Washington, DC and September 2013 in Havana.[70] As noted above, previous talks in 2009 did not lead to a resumption of direct mail service. The State Department reportedly characterized the September talks as "fruitful," and maintained in a statement that "the goal of the talks is for the United States and Cuba to work out the details for a pilot program to directly transport mail between the two countries."[71]

(...continued)

wha/rls/rm/2012/191935 htm.

[69] White House, "Remarks by the President at the Summit of the Americas Opening Ceremony," April 17, 2009.

[70] Since the early 1960s, mail to and from Cuba has arrived via third countries, which results in extensive delays in mail between the two countries. The Cuban Democracy Act of 1992 (P.L. 102-484, Title XVII, §1705(f)) has a provision requiring the U.S. Postal Service to take necessary actions to provide direct mail service to and from Cuba, including, in the absence of common carrier service between the 2 countries, the use of charter service providers. Past U.S. attempts to negotiate such service were rejected by Cuba, reportedly because Cuba wanted the issue to be part of a larger normalization of commercial air traffic. Both the Clinton and Bush Administrations had called for negotiations to restore direct mail service.

[71] Marc Frank, "U.S. and Cuba Talk about Resuming Direct Mail Service," *Reuters News*, September 17, 2013.

- After an 18-month hiatus, the Obama Administration resumed semi-annual migration talks on July 17, 2013 in Washington D.C., while another round was held in Havana on January 9, 2014. U.S. and Cuban officials issued positive statements after both rounds (for more details on the talks, see "Migration Issues" below).

- In September 2013, the United States and Cuba reportedly agreed to a preliminary procedure on air and maritime search and rescue. The U.S. Coast Guard led the U.S. delegation in Havana, and the talks reportedly stressed the importance of such cooperation to save lives of people in danger.[72] The January 2014 migration talks also included discussion of aviation safety and maritime search and rescue protocols.

In November 2013, President Obama and Secretary of State John Kerry both delivered remarks regarding U.S. policy toward Cuba. At a Democratic Party fundraising event on November 8 in Miami, President Obama maintained that with regard to policy toward Cuba, "we have to be creative ... we have to be thoughtful ... and we have to continue to update our policies." He contended that "the notion that the same polices that we put in place in 1961 would somehow still be as effective as they are today in the age of the Internet and Google and world travel doesn't make sense."[73] In a November 18, 2013 address on U.S.-Latin American relations at the Organization of American States, Secretary of State Kerry reiterated the President's remarks. He also maintained that the United States and Cuba "are finding some cooperation on common interests at this point in time," and that "we also welcome some of the changes that are taking place in Cuba which allow more Cubans to be able to travel freely and work for themselves." At the same time, however, the Secretary cautioned that changes in Cuba "should absolutely not blind us to the authoritarian reality of life for ordinary Cubans." He contended that "in a hemisphere where people can criticize their leaders without fear of arrest or violence, Cubans cannot. And if more does not change soon, it is clear that the 21st century will continued, unfortunately, to leave the Cuban people behind."[74]

Considerable international press focused on the handshake between President Obama and President Castro on December 10, 2013 at the memorial service for Nelson Mandela in South Africa. U.S. officials maintain that the handshake was not planned, but rather, that the focus of President Obama was on Mandela. Some analysts contend that the handshake could portend a sign of thawing relations while others maintain that sometimes a handshake is just a handshake. Critics of the Cuban government, including some Members of Congress, criticized the President for shaking hands with a leader with such a poor human rights record.

Human rights violations have remained a fundamental concern regarding Cuba under the Obama Administration. President Obama and the State Department have continued to issue statements expressing concern about violations as they occur, including the death of hunger strikers in 2010 and 2012 and targeted repression against dissidents and human rights. U.S. officials lauded the

---

[72] "Cuba, U.S. Reach Maritime Rescue Agreement," *Agence France Presse*, September 21, 2013; "Cuba, U.S. Agree to Preliminary Procedure for Aeronautical, Maritime Rescue," *Philippines News Agency*, September 22, 2013.

[73] The White House, Office of the Press Secretary, "Remarks by the President at a DSCC Fundraising Reception," Miami, Florida, November 8, 2013, available at http://www.whitehouse.gov/the-press-office/2013/11/08/remarks-president-dscc-fundraising-reception-0.

[74] U.S. Department of State, "Remarks on U.S. Policy in the Western Hemisphere," November 18, 2013, available at http://www.state.gov/secretary/remarks/2013/11/217680 htm.

release of dozens of Cuban political prisoners in 2010 and 2011, but maintain that their release has not changed the government's poor human rights record as it continues to resort to repeated short-term detentions.[75] In October 2013, Under Secretary of State for Political Affairs Wendy Sherman met with Berta Soler, spokesperson for the Ladies in White, and expressed concern over Cuba's "continued suppression of peaceful activities carried out by Damas de Blanco and other civil society groups."[76] In November 2013, President Obama met Berta Soler and another prominent Cuban dissident, Guillermo Fariñas, at an event in Miami, Florida, and Secretary of State Kerry, as noted above, addressed the OAS and reiterated concerns about human rights and freedom of expression in Cuba. In December 2013, the State Department issued a statement deploring "the Cuban government's harsh tactics to impede Cuban civil society's peaceful recognition of Human Rights Day."[77] In February 2014, the State Department issued a statement expressing deep concern about the "recent increase in arbitrary detentions, physical violence, and other abusive actions carried out by the Cuban government against peaceful human and civil rights advocates."[78]

Securing the release of Alan Gross from prison in Cuba also remains a top U.S. priority. The State Department maintains that it is using every appropriation channel to press for his release, including the Vatican. As noted by the State Department in early May 2014, Gross's continued well-being remains an impediment to more constructive bilateral relations.[79] (For more, see "Imprisonment of USAID Subcontractor since December 2009" below.)

Debate on the Direction of U.S. Policy

Over the years, although U.S. policy makers have agreed on the overall objectives of U.S. policy toward Cuba—to help bring democracy and respect for human rights to the island—there have been several schools of thought about how to achieve those objectives. Some have advocated a policy of keeping maximum pressure on the Cuban government until reforms are enacted, while continuing efforts to support the Cuban people. Others argue for an approach, sometimes referred to as constructive engagement, that would lift some U.S. sanctions that they believe are hurting the Cuban people, and move toward engaging Cuba in dialogue. Still others call for a swift normalization of U.S.-Cuban relations by lifting the U.S. embargo. Legislative initiatives introduced over the past decade have reflected these three policy approaches.

Over the past decade, there have been efforts in Congress to ease U.S. sanctions, with one or both houses at times approving amendments to appropriations measures that would have eased U.S. sanctions on Cuba. Until 2009, these provisions were stripped out of final enacted measures, in part because of presidential veto threats. In March 2009, Congress took action to ease some restrictions on travel to Cuba, marking the first time that Congress has eased Cuba sanctions since the approval of the Trade Sanctions Reform and Export Enhancement Act of 2000.

---

[75] U.S. Department of State, "The Path to Freedom Countering Repression and Strengthening Civil Society in Cuba," Testimony by Roberta S. Jacobson, Assistant Secretary, Bureau of Western Hemisphere Affairs, Senate Foreign Relations Committee, Subcommittee on the Western Hemisphere, June 7, 2012.

[76] U.S. Department of State, Daily Press Briefing, October 24, 2013.

[77] U.S. Department of State, "Crackdown on Cuban Civil Society's Human Rights Day Events," Press Statement, December 12, 2013.

[78] U.S. Department of State, "Detentions of Activists in Cuba," Press Statement, February 10, 2014.

[79] U.S. Department of State, "Continued Detention of Alan Gross," Press Statement, May 2, 2014.

In light of Fidel Castro's departure as head of government and the gradual economic changes being made by Raúl Castro, some observers called for a reexamination of U.S. policy toward Cuba. In this new context, two broad policy approaches have been advanced to contend with change in Cuba: an approach that maintains the U.S. dual-track policy of isolating the Cuban government while providing support to the Cuban people; and an approach aimed at influencing the attitudes of the Cuban government and Cuban society through increased contact and engagement.

In general, those who advocate easing U.S. sanctions on Cuba make several policy arguments. They assert that if the United States moderated its policy toward Cuba—through increased travel, trade, and dialogue—then the seeds of reform would be planted, which would stimulate forces for peaceful change on the island. They stress the importance to the United States of avoiding violent change in Cuba, with the prospect of a mass exodus to the United States. They argue that since the demise of Cuba's communist government does not appear imminent, even without Fidel Castro at the helm, the United States should espouse a more pragmatic approach in trying to bring about change in Cuba. Supporters of changing policy also point to broad international support for lifting the U.S. embargo, to the missed opportunities for U.S. businesses because of the unilateral nature of the embargo, and to the increased suffering of the Cuban people because of the embargo. Proponents of change also argue that the United States should be consistent in its policies with the world's few remaining communist governments, including China and Vietnam.

On the other side, opponents of changing U.S. policy maintain that the current two-track policy of isolating Cuba, but reaching out to the Cuban people through measures of support, is the best means for realizing political change in Cuba. They point out that the Cuban Liberty and Democratic Solidarity Act of 1996 sets forth the steps that Cuba needs to take in order for the United States to normalize relations. They argue that softening U.S. policy at this time without concrete Cuban reforms would boost the Castro government, politically and economically, and facilitate the survival of the communist regime. Opponents of softening U.S. policy argue that the United States should stay the course in its commitment to democracy and human rights in Cuba, and that sustained sanctions can work. Opponents of loosening U.S. sanctions further argue that Cuba's failed economic policies, not the U.S. embargo, are the causes of Cuba's difficult living conditions.

Issues in U.S.-Cuban Relations

For many years, Congress has played an active role in U.S. policy toward Cuba through the enactment of legislative initiatives and oversight on the many issues that comprise policy toward Cuba. These include U.S. restrictions on travel and remittances to Cuba; U.S. agricultural exports to Cuba with conditions; funding and oversight of U.S.-government sponsored democracy and human rights projects; the imprisonment of USAID subcontractor Alan Gross in Cuba since December 2009; funding and oversight for U.S.-government sponsored broadcasting to Cuba (Radio and TV Martí); terrorism issues; migration issues; bilateral anti-drug cooperation; and the status of Cuba's offshore oil development, including efforts to ensure adequate oil spill prevention, preparedness, and response efforts.

U.S. Restrictions on Travel and Remittances[80]

Restrictions on travel to Cuba have been a key and often contentious component of U.S. efforts to isolate the communist government of Fidel Castro for much of the past 50 years. Over time there have been numerous changes to the restrictions and for five years, from 1977 until 1982, there were no restrictions on travel. Restrictions on travel and remittances to Cuba are part of the CACR, the overall embargo regulations administered by the Treasury Department's Office of Foreign Assets Control (OFAC).

Under the George W. Bush Administration, enforcement of U.S. restrictions on Cuba travel increased, and restrictions on travel and on private remittances to Cuba were tightened. In 2003, the Administration eliminated travel for people-to-people educational exchanges that had begun under the Clinton Administration. In 2004, the Administration imposed further restrictions on travel, especially family travel and the provision of private humanitarian assistance to Cuba in the form of remittances and gift parcels.

Under the Obama Administration, Congress took legislative action in March 2009 easing restrictions on family travel (restoring the restrictions to as they were under the Clinton Administration) and on travel related to U.S. agricultural and medical sales to Cuba (P.L. 111-8, Sections 620 and 621 of Division D). In April 2009, the Obama Administration went further when the President announced that he was lifting *all* restrictions on family travel as well as restrictions on cash remittances to family members in Cuba.

In January 2011, the Obama Administration made a series of changes further easing restrictions on travel and remittances to Cuba. The measures (1) increased purposeful travel to Cuba related to religious, educational, and journalistic activities, including people-to-people travel exchanges; (2) allowed any U.S. person to send remittances to non-family members in Cuba and made it easier for religious institutions to send remittances for religious activities; and (3) allowed U.S. international airports to become eligible to provide services to licensed charter flights to and from Cuba.

In most respects, these new measures were similar to policies that were undertaken by the Clinton Administration in 1999, but were subsequently curtailed by the Bush Administration in 2003 and 2004. An exception is the expansion of airports to service licensed flights to and from Cuba. While the new travel regulations immediately went into effect for those categories of travel falling under a general license category, OFAC delayed processing applications for new travel categories requiring a specific license (such as people-to-people exchanges) until it updated and issued guidelines in April 2011.

The first people-to-people trips began in August 2011. In May 2012, the Treasury Department tightened its restrictions on people-to-people travel by making changes to its license guidelines. The revised guidelines require an organization applying for a people-to-people license to describe how the travel "would enhance contact with the Cuban people, and/or support civil society in Cuba, and/or promote the Cuban people's independence from Cuban authorities." The revised guidelines also require specification on how meetings with prohibited officials of the Cuban government would advance purposeful travel by enhancing contact with the Cuban people,

---

[80] For additional information, see CRS Report RL31139, *Cuba: U.S. Restrictions on Travel and Remittances*, by Mark P. Sullivan.

supporting civil society, or promoting independence from Cuban authorities.[81] In September 2012, various press reports cited a slowdown in the Treasury Department's approval or reapproval of licenses for people-to-people travel since the agency had issued new guidelines in May. Companies conducting such programs complained that the delay in the licenses was forcing them to cancel trips and even to lay off staff.[82] By early October 2012, however, companies conducting the people-to-people travel maintained that they were once again receiving license approvals.

In early April 2013, some Members of Congress strongly criticized singers Beyoncé Knowles-Carter and her husband Shawn Carter, better known as Jay-Z, for traveling to Cuba. Members were concerned that the trip, as described in the press, was primarily for tourism, which would be contrary to U.S. law and regulations. The Treasury Department stated that the two singers were participating in an authorized people-to-people exchange trip organized by a group licensed by OFAC to conduct such trips (pursuant to 31 C.F.R. 515.565(b)(2) of the Cuban Assets Control Regulations). Some Members also criticized the singers for not meeting with those who have been oppressed by the Cuban government.

On April 30, 2013, 59 House Democrats sent a letter to President Obama lauding the President for his 2009 action lifting restrictions on family travel and remittances, and for his 2011 action easing restrictions on some categories of travel, including people-to-people travel. The Members also called for the President to further use his "executive authority to allow all current categories of permissible travel, including people-to-people travel," to be carried out under a general license (instead of having to apply to Treasury Department for a specific license). Such an action, according to the Members, would increase opportunities for engagement and help Cubans create more jobs and opportunities to expand their independence from the Cuban government.

Major arguments made for lifting the Cuba travel ban altogether are that it abridges the rights of ordinary Americans to travel; it hinders efforts to influence conditions in Cuba and may be aiding Castro by helping restrict the flow of information; and Americans can travel to other countries with communist or authoritarian governments. Major arguments in opposition to lifting the Cuba travel ban are that more American travel would support Castro's rule by providing his government with potentially millions of dollars in hard currency; that there are legal provisions allowing travel to Cuba for humanitarian purposes that are used by thousands of Americans each year; and that the President should be free to restrict travel for foreign policy reasons.

Legislative Activity. In the 112th Congress, interest on the issue of Cuba travel and remittances continued. Legislation was introduced to roll back some of the easing of restrictions and some bills were introduced to further ease travel restrictions or lift them altogether, but ultimately none of the measures were enacted.

In the 113th Congress, both the House and Senate versions of the FY2014 Financial Services and General Government appropriations measure, H.R. 2786 and S. 1371, had different provisions that would have tightened and eased travel restrictions respectively, but none of these provisions were included in the FY2014 omnibus appropriations measure, H.R. 3547 (P.L. 113-76), signed into law January 17, 2014. The House version of the FY2014 Financial Services and General

---

[81] U.S. Department of the Treasury, OFAC, "Comprehensive Guidelines for License Applications to Engage in Travel-Related Transactions Involving Cuba," Revised May 10, 2012.

[82] Damien Cave, "Licensing Rules Slow Tours to Cuba," *New York Times*, September 16, 2012; Paul Haven, "U.S. Travel Outfits Say Rules for Legal Travel to Cuba Getting Tighter," *Associated Press*, September 13, 2012.

Government appropriations measure, H.R. 2786 (H.Rept. 113-172), would have prohibited FY2014 funding used "to approve, license, facilitate, authorize, or otherwise allow" people-to-people travel to Cuba, which the Obama Administration authorized in 2011. In contrast, the Senate version of the measure, S. 1371 (S.Rept. 113-80), would have expanded the current general license for professional research and meetings in Cuba to allow U.S. groups to sponsor and organize conferences in Cuba, but only if specifically related to disaster prevention, emergency preparedness, and natural resource protection. (For additional information see CRS Report R43352, *Financial Services and General Government (FSGG): FY2014 Appropriations.*)

In addition, several legislative initiatives have been introduced in the 113th Congress that would lift all travel restrictions: H.R. 871 (Rangel) would lift travel restrictions; H.R. 873 (Rangel) would lift restrictions on U.S. agricultural exports as well as travel restrictions; and H.R. 214 (Serrano), H.R. 872 (Rangel), and H.R. 1917 (Rush) would lift the overall embargo on Cuba, including travel restrictions.

U.S. Agricultural Exports and Sanctions

U.S. commercial agricultural exports to Cuba have been allowed for more than a decade, but with numerous restrictions and licensing requirements. The 106th Congress passed the Trade Sanctions Reform and Export Enhancement Act of 2000 or TSRA (P.L. 106-387, Title IX) that allows for one-year export licenses for selling agricultural commodities to Cuba, although no U.S. government assistance, foreign assistance, export assistance, credits, or credit guarantees are available to finance such exports. TSRA also denies exporters access to U.S. private commercial financing or credit; all transactions must be conducted in cash in advance or with financing from third countries.

Cuba has purchased about $4.8 billion in products from the United States since 2001, largely agricultural products. U.S. exports to Cuba rose from about $7 million in 2001 to $404 million in 2004 and to a high of $712 million in 2008, far higher than in previous years, in part because of the rise in food prices and because of Cuba's increased food needs in the aftermath of several hurricanes and tropical storms that severely damaged the country's agricultural sector. From 2002 through 2010, the United States was the largest supplier of food and agricultural products to Cuba. In 2011, Brazil became Cuba's largest agricultural supplier, but this shifted back again to the United States in 2012.[83]

U.S. exports to Cuba declined considerably from 2009 through 2011, amounting to $363 million in 2010 and 2011 (see **Figure 5**).[84] In 2012, the level of U.S. exports to Cuba rose to $464 million, a 28% increase over the previous year, but still lower than export levels to Cuba in 2008 and 2009. Part of the increase in 2012 can be attributed to an increase in Cuba's import needs because of damage to the agricultural sector in eastern Cuba caused by Hurricane Sandy in October. In 2013, U.S. exports to Cuba fell to $358 million, a decline of about 23% from the previous year. In the first quarter of 2014, U.S. exports to amounted to $133 million, about 8% less than the same period in 2013.

---

[83] Global Trade Atlas, derived by looking at reporting partners' exports to Cuba.

[84] The U.S. trade statistics cited in this report are from the Department of Commerce, as presented by Global Trade Atlas.

Looking at the composition of U.S. exports to Cuba in recent years, the leading products have been poultry, soybean oilcake, corn, and soybeans. Among the reasons for the overall decline in U.S. exports to Cuba in recent years, analysts cite Cuba's shortage of hard currency; credits and other arrangements offered by other governments to purchase their countries' products; and Cuba's perception that its efforts to motivate U.S. companies, organizations, local and state officials, and Members of Congress to push for change in U.S. sanctions policy toward Cuba have been ineffective.[85]

Figure 5. U.S. Exports to Cuba, 2001-2013

(U.S. $ millions)

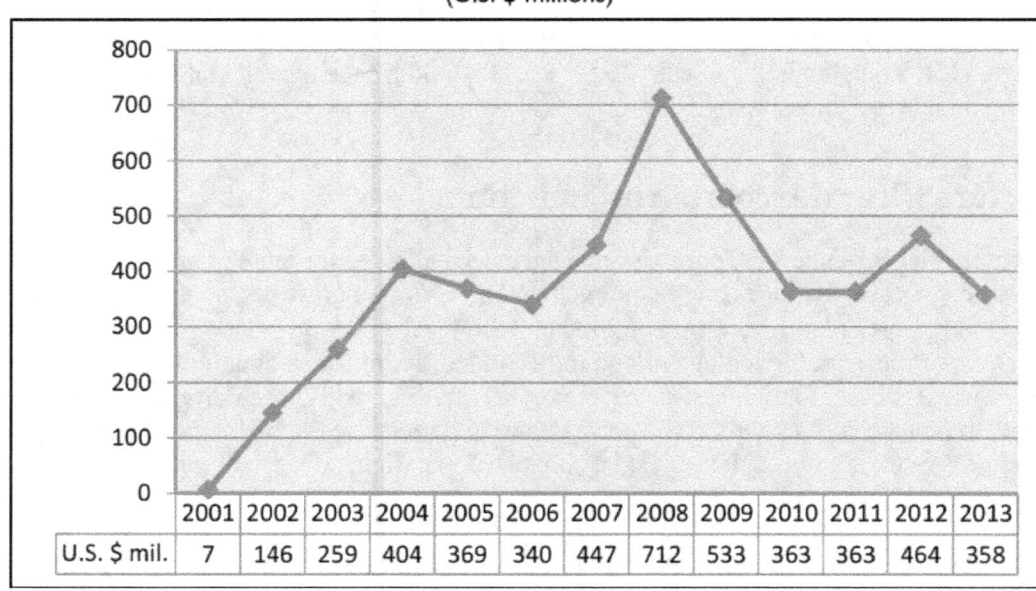

	2001	2002	2003	2004	2005	2006	2007	2008	2009	2010	2011	2012	2013
U.S. $ mil.	7	146	259	404	369	340	447	712	533	363	363	464	358

Source: Created by CRS using information from the Global Trade Atlas, which uses data from the U.S. Department of Commerce.

The U.S. International Trade Commission (USITC) produced a study in 2007 analyzing the effects of both U.S. government financing restrictions for agricultural exports to Cuba and U.S. travel restrictions on the level of U.S. agricultural sales to Cuba.[86] At the time of the study, the U.S. share of various Cuban agricultural imports was estimated to range from 0-99% depending on the commodity. If U.S. financing restrictions were lifted, the study estimated that the U.S. share of Cuban agricultural, fish, and forest products imports would rise to between one-half and two-thirds. According to the study, if travel restrictions for all U.S. citizens were lifted, the influx of U.S. tourists would be significant in the short term and would boost demand for imported agricultural products, particularly high-end products for the tourist sector. If both financing and travel restrictions were lifted, the study found that the largest gains in U.S. exports to Cuba would be for fresh fruits and vegetables, milk powder, processed foods, wheat, and dry beans.

---

[85] Juan Tamayo, "Big Drop in U.S. Agricultural Sales to Cuba," *Miami Herald*, July 29, 2010; Marc Frank, "U.S. Food Sales to Cuba Continued Decline in 2011," *Reuters News*, February 22, 2012; U.S.-Cuba Trade and Economic Council, Inc. "Economic Eye on Cuba," April 2014.

[86] USITC, *U.S. Agricultural Sales to Cuba: Certain Economic Effects of U.S. Restrictions*, USITC Publication 3932, July 2007, available at http://www.usitc.gov/ext_relations/news_release/2007/er0719ee1.htm.

In 2009, the USITC issued a working paper that updated the agency's 2007 study on U.S. agricultural sales to Cuba. The update concluded that if U.S. restrictions on financing and travel were lifted in 2008, U.S. agricultural exports to Cuba would have increased between $216 million and $478 million and the U.S. share of Cuba's agricultural imports would have increased from 38% to between 49% and 64%.[87] Among the U.S. agricultural products that would have benefited the most were wheat, rice, beef, pork, processed foods, and fish products.

In general, some groups favor further easing restrictions on agricultural exports to Cuba. U.S. agribusiness companies that support the removal of restrictions on agricultural exports to Cuba believe that U.S. farmers are unable to capitalize on a market so close to the United States. Those who support the lifting of financing restrictions contend such an action would help smaller U.S. companies increase their exports to Cuba more rapidly. Opponents of further easing restrictions on agricultural exports to Cuba maintain that U.S. policy does not deny such sales to Cuba, as evidenced by the large amount of sales since 2001.

Legislative Activity. Over the past several years, there have been legislative efforts to further ease restrictions on agricultural exports to Cuba. For FY2010 and FY2011, Congress included a provision in omnibus appropriations measures (Division C, Section 619 of P.L. 111-117, and continued by reference in Division B, Section 1101 of P.L. 112-10) that temporarily overturned OFAC's 2005 clarification that TSRA's requirement for "payment of cash in advance" meant that the payment for the agricultural goods had to be received prior to the shipment of the goods from the port at which they were loaded in the United States. U.S. agricultural exporters and some Members of Congress had objected that OFAC's 2005 action constituted a new sanction that violated the intent of TSRA, and jeopardized million in agricultural sales. The legislative provisions cited above redefined payment of cash in advance for FY2010 and FY2011 to mean that payment was to be received before the transfer of title to, and control of, the exported items to the Cuban purchaser. This essentially meant that payment could occur before a shipment was offloaded in Cuba, rather than before an export shipment left a U.S. port.

For FY2012, Congress did not include a similar provision in the Consolidated Appropriations Act, 2012 (P.L. 112-74). While the Senate Appropriations Committee-approved version of the FY2012 Financial Services appropriations measure (S. 1573) had a provision that would have continued the definition of "payment of cash in advance" utilized in FY2010 and FY2011, this was not included in the final omnibus legislation. The Senate bill also contained another Cuba provision that would have prohibited restrictions on direct transfers from a Cuban financial institution to a U.S. financial institution in payment for licensed exports to Cuba. This provision as well was not included in the omnibus appropriations legislation.

To date in the 113th Congress, one bill has been introduced that includes measures to facilitate the export of U.S. agricultural products to Cuba, H.R. 873 (Rangel), while three other bills that would lift the overall embargo, H.R. 214 (Serrano), H.R. 872 (Rangel), and H.R. 1917 (Rush), would lift restrictions and licensing requirements on U.S. agricultural exports to Cuba.

---

[87] USITC, *U.S. Agricultural Sales to Cuba: Certain Economic Effects of U.S. Restrictions, An Update,* Office of Industries Working Paper, by Jonathan R. Coleman, No. ID-22, June 2009, available at http://www.usitc.gov/publications/332/working_papers/ID-22.pdf.

Trademark Sanction[88]

For some 15 years, the United States has imposed a trademark sanction specifically related to Cuba. A provision in the FY1999 omnibus appropriations measure (§211 of Division A, Title II, P.L. 105-277, signed into law October 21, 1998) prevents the United States from accepting payment for trademark registrations and renewals from Cuban nationals that were used in connection with a business or assets in Cuba that were confiscated, unless the original owner of the trademark has consented. The provision prohibits U.S. courts from recognizing such trademarks without the consent of the original owner. The measure was enacted because of a dispute between the French spirits company, Pernod Ricard, and the Bermuda-based Bacardi Ltd. Pernod Ricard entered into a joint venture in 1993 with the Cuban government to produce and export Havana Club rum. Bacardi maintains that it holds the right to the Havana Club name because in 1995 it entered into an agreement for the Havana Club trademark with the Arechabala family, who had originally produced the rum until its assets and property were confiscated by the Cuban government in 1960. Although Pernod Ricard cannot market Havana Club in the United States because of the trade embargo, it wants to protect its future distribution rights should the embargo be lifted.

The European Union initiated World Trade Organization (WTO) dispute settlement proceedings in June 2000, maintaining that the U.S. law violates the Agreement on Trade-Related Aspects of Intellectual Property (TRIPS). In January 2002, the WTO ultimately found that the trademark sanction violated WTO provisions on national treatment and most-favored-nation obligations in the TRIPS Agreement.[89] On March 28, 2002, the United States agreed that it would come into compliance with the WTO ruling through legislative action by January 3, 2003.[90] That deadline was extended several times since no legislative action had been taken to bring Section 211 into compliance with the WTO ruling. On July 1, 2005, however, in an EU-U.S. bilateral agreement, the EU agreed that it would not request authorization to retaliate at that time, but reserved the right to do so at a future date, and the United States agreed not to block a future EU request.[91] In June 2013, EU officials reportedly raised the issue of U.S. compliance at a WTO Dispute Settlement Body meeting, maintaining that there has been enough time for the United States to settle the issue, while U.S. officials maintained that relevant bills were before the U.S. Congress.[92]

On August 3, 2006, the U.S. Patent and Trademark Office announced that Cuba's Havana Club trademark registration was "cancelled/expired," a week after OFAC had denied a Cuban government company the license that it needed to renew the registration of the trademark.[93] On

---

[88] For background information, see archived CRS Report RS21764, *Restricting Trademark Rights of Cubans: WTO Decision and Congressional Response*, by Margaret Mikyung Lee, March 9, 2004.

[89] For background, see archived CRS Report RL32014, *WTO Dispute Settlement: Status of U.S. Compliance in Pending Cases*, by Jeanne J. Grimmett, April 23, 2012.

[90] "U.S., EU Agree on Deadline for Complying with Section 211 WTO Finding," *Inside U.S. Trade*, April 12, 2002.

[91] World Trade Organization (WTO), "United States—Section 211 Omnibus Appropriations Act of 1998, Understanding between the European Communities and the United States," WT/DC176/16, July 1, 2005; WTO, Dispute Settlement Body, "Minutes of Meeting, Held in the Centre William Rappard on 20 July 2005," WT/DSB/M/194, August 26, 2005; and "Japan, EU Suspend WTO Retaliation Against U.S. in Two Cases," *Inside U.S. Trade*, July 15, 2005.

[92] "EU, Cuba Spar with U.S. Over 'Havana Club' Rum," *Agence France Presse*, June 25, 2013.

[93] "PTO Cancels Cuban 'Havana Club' Mark; Bacardi Set to Sell Rum Under Same Mark," *International Trade Daily*, August 10, 2006.

March 29, 2011, the U.S. Court of Appeals of the District of Columbia upheld the decision to deny the renewal of the trademark,[94] while in May 2012, the U.S. Supreme Court declined to hear the case, effectively letting stand the denial to renew the trademark.[95]

Bacardi began marketing Havana Club rum in the United States in 2006 in limited quantities in Florida, and Pernod Ricard filed suit that the representation of the origin of the rum was misleading. In April 2010, a U.S. District Court in Delaware ruled in Bacardi's favor that the labeling was not misleading, and this was reaffirmed by a U.S. Court of Appeals on August 4, 2011.[96]

Legislative Activity. In Congress, two different approaches have been advocated for a number of years to bring Section 211 into compliance with the WTO ruling. Some want a narrow fix in which Section 211 would be amended so that it applies to all persons claiming rights in trademarks confiscated by Cuba, whatever their nationality, instead of being limited to designated nationals, meaning Cuban nationals. Advocates of this approach argue that it would treat all holders of U.S. trademarks equally. Others want Section 211 repealed altogether. They argue that the law endangers over 5,000 trademarks of over 500 U.S. companies registered in Cuba.[97] The House Committee on the Judiciary held a March 3, 2010, hearing on the "Domestic and International Trademark Implications of HAVANA CLUB and Section 211 of the Omnibus Appropriations Act of 2009," which featured proponents of both legislative approaches. (See http://judiciary.house.gov/hearings/hear_100303.html.)

Several legislative initiatives were introduced during the 112th Congress reflecting these two approaches to bring Section 211 into compliance with the WTO ruling, but no action was taken on these measures. In the 113th Congress, identical bills H.R. 778 (Issa) and S. 647 (Nelson) would apply the narrow fix so that the trademark sanction would apply to all nationals, while four broader bills lifting U.S. sanctions on Cuba—H.R. 214 (Serrano); H.R. 872 (Rangel); H.R. 873 (Rangel); and H.R. 1917 (Rush)—each have a provision that would repeal the trademark sanction. The July 2005 EU-U.S. bilateral agreement, in which the EU agreed not to retaliate against the United States, but reserved the right to do so at a later date, has reduced pressure on Congress to take action to comply with the WTO ruling.

U.S. Funding to Support Democracy and Human Rights

Since 1996, the United States has provided assistance—through the U.S. Agency for International Development (USAID), the State Department, and the National Endowment for Democracy (NED)—to increase the flow of information on democracy, human rights, and free enterprise to Cuba.

USAID and State Department efforts are largely funded through Economic Support Funds (ESF) in the annual foreign operations appropriations bill. From FY1996 to FY2014, Congress appropriated some $264 million in funding for Cuba democracy efforts. In recent years, this

---

[94] "Pernod Ricard: Havana Club International Encouraged by Dissenting Opinion of Judge Silberman Will Seek Rehearing by Full Court of Appeals," *Business Wire*, March 29, 2011.

[95] "Supreme Court Rejects Havana Club Cert Petition," *International Trade Reporter*, May 14, 2012.

[96] Anandashankar Mazumdar, "Court Rejects Claim that 'Havana Club' Ruling Erred in Discounting Survey Evidence," *International Trade Reporter*, August 18, 2011.

[97] "USA-Engage Joins Cuba Fight," *Cuba Trader*, April 1, 2002.

included $45.3 million for FY2008 and $20 million in each fiscal year from FY2009 through FY2012, $19.3 million in FY2013, and $20 million in FY2014. The Administration's FY2015 request is for $20 million.

Generally, as provided in appropriations measures, ESF has to be obligated within two years. In earlier years, USAID received the majority of this funding, but the State Department also received funding beginning in FY2004 and in recent years has been allocated slightly more funding than USAID. The State Department generally has transferred a portion of the Cuba assistance that it administers to NED. For FY2014, however, Congress stipulated that not less than $7.5 million shall be provided directly to NED while not more than $10 million shall be administered by the State Department; Congress also stipulated that no ESF appropriated under the Act may be obligated by USAID for any new programs or activities in Cuba (P.L. 113-76).

USAID's Cuba program has supported a variety of U.S.-based non-governmental organizations with the goals of promoting a rapid, peaceful transition to democracy, helping develop civil society, and building solidarity with Cuba's human rights activists. USAID maintains on its website that current USAID program partners are: Foundation for Human Rights in Cuba, $3.4 million (2011-2014); Grupo de Apoyo a la Democracia, $3.5 million (2012-2015); International Relief and Development, $3.5 million (2011-2014); International Republican Institute, $3 million (2012-2015); National Democratic Institute, $2.3 million (2011-2014); New America Foundation, $4.3 million (2012-2015); and Pan-American Development Foundation, $3.9 million (2011-2014). (See USAID's Cuba program website at http://www.usaid.gov/where-we-work/latin-american-and-caribbean/cuba.)

FY2012. The Administration requested $20 million in ESF for FY2012 with the promotion of democratic principles as the core goal of assistance, and Congress supported the full amount in the conference report to the FY2012 Consolidated Appropriations Act (H.Rept. 112-331 to H.R. 2055, P.L. 112-74). The budget request stated that there was an increased effort to manage programs more transparently, focus efforts on Cuba, and widen the scope of the civic groups receiving supports. According to the Administration's request, U.S. assistance would strengthen a range of independent elements of Cuban civil society, including associations and labor groups, marginalized groups, youth, legal associations, and women's networks. The programs would be designed to increase the capacity for community involvement of civil society organizations and networking among the groups. The program would also support Cuban efforts to document human rights violations, provide humanitarian assistance to political prisoners and their families, and build leadership skills of civil society leaders. Finally, the budget request maintained that U.S. assistance also would support the dissemination of information regarding market economies and economic rights.

The Senate Appropriations Committee-reported version of the FY2012 Department of State, Foreign Operations, and Related Programs Appropriations bill, S. 1601 (S.Rept. 112-85), would have provided $15 million in ESF for Cuba ($5 million less than the request), including humanitarian and democracy assistance, support for economic reform, private sector initiatives, and human rights. In its report to the bill, the committee maintained that it expected that funds would be made available, and programs carried out, in a transparent manner. The committee also would have directed that the USAID Administrator provide regular updates to the committee on the number of Cubans who receive assistance and the types of assistance. In contrast to the Senate bill, a draft House Appropriations Committee bill and report (marked up by the Subcommittee on State, Foreign Operations, and Relations Programs on July 27, 2011) would have recommended $20 million in ESF for Cuba (the full Administration's request), and would have directed that the funds be used only for democracy-building, and not for business promotion, economic reform, social development or other purposes expressly authorized by Section 109(a) of the Cuban Liberty and Democratic Solidarity Act of 1996 (P.L. 104-114). (See the draft committee report, available at http://appropriations.house.gov/UploadedFiles/FY12-SFOPSCombinedReport-CSBA.pdf.)

As notified to Congress in May 2013, of the $20 million in Cuba projects for FY2012, USAID will administer $9.45 million; the State Department's Bureau of Democracy, Human Rights, and Labor will administer $9.85 million (of which $4 million will be transferred to NED); and the State Department's Bureau of Western Hemisphere Affairs will administer $0.7 million. In terms of the types of programs funded, $2.96 million will be used to support human rights initiatives; $13.07 million will be used for civil society and media programs; and $3.97 million for be used for program support.

FY2013. For FY2013, the Administration requested $15 million in ESF for human rights and democracy programs for Cuba. According to the request, "U.S. assistance will continue to support human rights and civil society initiatives that promote basic freedoms, particularly freedom of expression. Programs will continue to provide humanitarian assistance to prisoners of conscience and their families, as well as strengthen independent Cuban civil society, and promote the flow of uncensored information to, from, and within the island."[98]

The Senate Appropriations Committee-reported version of the FY2013 State Department, Foreign Operations, and Related Programs Appropriations Act, S. 3241 (S.Rept. 112-172), would have provided $15 million in ESF for Cuba (the same as the Administration's request), including "for humanitarian assistance, support for economic reform, private sector initiatives, democracy, and human rights." In contrast, the House Appropriations Committee-reported version of the bill, H.R. 5857 (H.Rept. 112-94), would have provided $20 million in ESF ($5 million more than the Administration's request), but would transfer and merge the aid with funds available to the National Endowment for Democracy "to promote democracy and strengthen civil society in Cuba." The report to the House bill maintained that assistance "shall not be used for business promotion, economic reform, social development, or other purposes not expressly authorized by section 109(a)" of the Cuban Liberty and Democratic Solidarity Act (P.L. 104-114).

Congress did not complete action on FY2013 appropriations before the beginning of the fiscal year, but in September 2012, it approved a continuing resolution (H.J.Res. 117, P.L. 112-175) that continued FY2013 funding through March 27, 2013, at the same rate for projects and activities in FY2012, plus an across-the-board increase of 0.612%, although specific country accounts were left to the discretion of responsible agencies. On March 21, 2013, Congress completed action on full-year FY2013 appropriations with the approval of H.R. 933 (P.L. 113-6). This continued FY2013 funding for Cuba democracy programs but funding was also affected by budget sequestration cutbacks set forth in the Budget Control Act of 2011 (P.L. 112-25), as amended by the American Taxpayer Relief Act (P.L. 112-240). Ultimately, $19.283 million was appropriated for FY2013 Cuba democracy funding.

FY2014. For FY2014, the Administration again requested $15 million in ESF for Cuba human rights and democracy projects. According to the budget request, U.S. aid will strengthen

---

[98] U.S. Department of State, *Congressional Budget Justification for Foreign Operations, FY2013, Annex: Regional Perspectives*, April 3, 2012, p. 768.

independent Cuban civil by supporting initiatives that promote democracy, human rights, and fundamental freedoms, particularly freedom of expression. Programs will also provide humanitarian assistance to victims of political repression and their families and promote the flow of uncensored information to, from, and within Cuba.[99]

The Senate Appropriations Committee version of the FY2014 Department of State, Foreign Operations, and Related Programs Appropriations Act, S. 1372 (S.Rept. 113-81, reported July 25, 2013), would have provided that ESF assistance appropriated for Cuba only be made available "for humanitarian assistance and to support the development of private business." The House Appropriations Committee version of the bill, H.R. 2855 (H.Rept. 113-185, reported July 30, 2013) would have provided that $20 million in ESF assistance ($5 million more than the Administration's request) be transferred to the National Endowment for Democracy "to promote democracy and strengthen civil society in Cuba." The report to the House bill stated that such assistance provided for Cuba "shall not used for business promotion, economic reform, social development, or other purposes not expressly authorized by section 109(a)" of the of the Cuban Liberty and Democratic Solidarity Act (P.L. 104-114).

Congress ultimately completed action on FY2014 appropriations in January 2014 when it enacted the Consolidated Appropriations Act, 2014, H.R. 3547 (P.L. 113-76), signed into law January 17, 2014. As noted above, the stated that up to $17.5 million should be made available in ESF for programs and activities in Cuba and stipulated that no ESF appropriated under the Act may be obligated by USAID for any new programs or activities in Cuba. The joint explanatory statement to the bill states that of the $17.5 million, not less than $7.5 million shall be provided directly to NED, and not more than $10 million shall be administered by the State Department's Bureau of Democracy, Human Rights, and Labor and Bureau of Western Hemisphere Affairs. Ultimately, however, the Administration is providing an estimated $20 million in ESF for FY2014 Cuba democracy programs, $5 million more than requested and $2.5 million more than the $17.5 million implied by P.L. 113-76 and its joint explanatory statement.

FY2015. The Administration requested $20 million in ESF for Cuba democracy program in 2015, the same as being provided in FY2014. According to the foreign aid budget request: "U.S. assistance will support civil society initiatives that promote democracy, human rights and fundamental freedoms, particularly freedom of expression. Programs will provide humanitarian assistance to victims of political repression and their families, strengthen independent Cuban civil society, and promote the flow of uncensored information to, from, and within the island." The request described three key aspects of the program: (1) working with independent elements of civil society to increase the capacity for community involvement, build networking among civil society organizations, and build the leadership skills of a future generation of civil society leaders; (2) facilitating information sharing into and out of Cuba, as well as among civil society groups on the island, including through the use of new technology; and (3) supporting Cuban-led efforts to document human rights violations, and providing humanitarian assistance to victims of political repression and their families.

National Endowment for Democracy. NED is not a U.S. government agency but an independent nongovernmental organization that receives U.S. government funding. Its Cuba program is funded by the organization's regular appropriations by Congress as well as by funding

---

[99] U.S. Department of State, Congressional Budget Justification for Foreign Operations FY2014, Annex: Regional Perspectives.

from the State Department. Until FY2008, NED's democratization assistance for Cuba had been funded largely through the annual Commerce, Justice, and State (CJS) appropriations measure, but is now funded through the State Department, Foreign Operations and Related Agencies appropriations measure. As noted above, for FY2014, Congress stipulated that not less than $7.5 million of democracy assistance for Cuba be provided directly to NED for activities and programs in Cuba. Depending on how much actually flows to NED, this would be at least two times the $3.4 million that NED spent for its Cuba projects in FY2013.

According to NED, its Cuba funding in recent years has been as follows: $1.4 million in FY2008; $1.5 million in FY2009; $2.4 million in FY2010; $1.65 million in FY2011; and $2.6 million in FY2012. In FY2013, NED provided $3.4 million as follows: Afro-Cuban Alliance, Inc. (two projects); Asociación de Iberoamericanos por la Libertad; Asociación Diario de Cuba; Center for a Free Cuba; Centro de Investigación y Capacitación de Emprendedores Sociales Asociación Civil; Centro Democracia y Comunidad; Centro para la Apertura y el Desarrollo de América Latina; Clovek v tisni, o.p.s. – People in Need; Committee for Free and Democratic Cuban Unions, Incorporated; Cuban Democratic Directorate; Cuban Soul Foundation; Cubanet News Inc.; Fundación Hispano Cubana; Global Rights (two projects); Grupo Internacional para la Responsibilidad Social Corporativa en Cuba (two projects); Instituto Cubano por la Libertad de Expresión y Prensa; Instituto Político para La Libertad Perú; International Platform for Human Rights in Cuba; Lech Walesa Institute; Observatorio Cubano de Derechos Humanos; Outreach Aid to the Americas, Inc.; People in Peril Association, CVO; Plataforma de Integración Cubana; Civic Education (three projects); Human Rights; and Rule of Law (two projects).[100]

Oversight of U.S. Democracy Assistance to Cuba

GAO has issued several reports since 2006 examining USAID and State Department democracy programs for Cuba. In 2006, GAO issued a report examining programs from 1996 through 2005, and concluded that the U.S. program had significant problems and needed better management and oversight. According to GAO, internal controls, for both the awarding of Cuba program grants and oversight of grantees, "do not provide adequate assurance that the funds are being used properly and that grantees are in compliance with applicable law and regulations."[101] Investigative news reports on the program maintained that high shipping costs and lax oversight had diminished its effectiveness.[102]

GAO issued a second report in 2008 examining USAID's Cuba democracy program.[103] The report lauded the steps that USAID had taken since 2006 to address problems with its Cuba program and improve oversight of the assistance. These included awarding all grants competitively since 2006, hiring more staff for the program office since January 2008, and contracting for financial services in April 2008 to enhance oversight of grantees. The GAO report also noted that USAID had worked to strengthen program oversight through pre-award and follow-up reviews, improving

---

[100] See more on the FY2013 projects available from NED's website at http://www.ned.org/where-we-work/latin-america-and-caribbean/cuba.

[101] U.S. Government Accountability Office (GAO), U.S. Democracy Assistance for Cuba Needs Better Management and Oversight, GAO-07-147, November 2006.

[102] Oscar Corral, "Federal Program to Help Democracy in Cuba Falls Short of Mark," *Miami Herald*, November 14, 2006, and "Is U.S. Aid Reaching Castro Foes?" *Miami Herald*, November 15, 2006.

[103] U.S. GAO, *Foreign Assistance: Continued Efforts Needed to Strengthen USAID's Oversight of U.S. Democracy Assistance for Cuba*, GAO-09-165, November 2008.

grantee internal controls and implementation plans, and providing guidance and monitoring about permitted types of assistance and cost sharing. The 2008 GAO report also maintained, however, that USAID had not staffed the Cuba program to the level needed for effective grant oversight. GAO recommended that USAID (1) ensure that its Cuba program office is staffed at the level that is needed to fully implement planned monitoring activities; and (2) periodically assess the Cuba program's overall efforts to address and reduce grantee risks, especially regarding internal controls, procurement practices, expenditures, and compliance with laws and regulations.

More recently, in January 2013, GAO issued its third report on Cuba democracy programs.[104] The report concluded that USAID had improved its performance and financial monitoring of implementing partners' use of program funds, but found that the State Department's financial monitoring had gaps. Both agencies were reported to be taking steps to improve financial monitoring. GAO recommended that the Secretary of State take two actions to strengthen the agency's ability to monitor the use of Cuba democracy program funds: use a risk-based approach for program audits that considers specific indicators for program partners; and obtain sufficient information to approve implementing partners' use of subpartners.

"Cuban Twitter" Controversy. In early April 2014, an *Associated Press* investigative report alleged that USAID, as part of its democracy promotion efforts for Cuba, had established a "Cuban Twitter" known as ZunZuneo, a communications network designed as a "covert" program "to undermine" Cuba's communist government built with "secret shell companies" and financed through foreign banks. According to the press report, the project, which was used by thousands of Cubans, lasted more than two years until it ended in 2012.[105] USAID, which strongly contested the report, issued a statement and facts about the ZunZuneo program. It maintained that program was not "covert," but rather that, just as in other places works where it is not always welcome, the agency maintained a "discreet profile" on the project to minimize risk to staff and partners and work safely.[106] Some Members of Congress strongly criticized USAID for not providing sufficient information to Congress about the program when funding was appropriated, while other Members strongly defended the agency and the program.

Imprisonment of USAID Subcontractor since December 2009

As noted earlier, USAID subcontractor Alan Gross has been imprisoned in Cuba since December 2009 for his work on a Cuba democracy project designed to provide Cuba's Jewish community with communication equipment for wireless Internet connectivity. In March 2011, he was convicted by a Cuban court in March 2011 and sentenced to 15 years in prison. Gross has remained in prison despite numerous calls for his release on humanitarian grounds by Members of Congress, the Obama Administration, and many other religious and human rights groups. His continued imprisonment has been an impediment to an improvement in U.S.-Cuban relations. In 2012, Cuba began linking the release of Alan Gross to the release of the so-called "Cuban five",

---

[104] U.S. GAO, *Cuba Democracy Assistance, USAID's Program is Improved, but State Could Better Monitor Its Implementing Partners*, GAO-13-285, January 2013.

[105] Desmond Butler, Jack Gillum, and Alberto Arce, "U.S. Secretly Created 'Cuban Twitter' to Stir Unrest," *Associated Press*, April 3, 2014.

[106] USAID, "Statement in Reference to the Associated Press Article on "Cuba Twitter" on April 3, 2014," Press Statement, April 3, 2014; "Eight Fact About ZunZuneo," April 7, 2014, available at http://blog.usaid.gov/2014/04/eight-facts-about-zunzuneo/.

who were convicted in the United States for espionage in 2001 (see "Cuban Five" below). The United States rejects such linkage, maintaining there is no equivalence between the cases.[107]

Gross was working as a USAID subcontractor for Development Alternatives Inc. (DAI), a Bethesda-based company that had received a contract from USAID to help support Cuban civil society organizations. As part of the project, Gross installed broadband Internet connections for three Jewish communities in the cities of Havana, Camagüey, and Santiago de Cuba. He was arrested on December 4, 2009, at Jose Martí International Airport in Havana when he was planning to leave the country after his fifth trip to Cuba under his subcontract with DAI. According to a statement at the time by DAI, Gross "was working with a peaceful, non-dissident civic group—a religious and cultural group recognized by the Cuban government—to improve its ability to communicate with its members across the island and overseas."[108]

After 14 months in prison, a Cuban court in Havana officially charged Gross on February 4, 2011, with "actions against the independence and territorial integrity of the state" pursuant to Article 91 of Cuba's Penal Code. After a two-day trial in March 2011, Gross was convicted and sentenced to 15 years in prison. Gross's lawyer had asked for the Cuban government to release Gross as a humanitarian gesture, maintaining that his health continued to deteriorate and noting that his elderly mother had been recently diagnosed with lung cancer, and his daughter was recovering from cancer treatment. Cuba's Supreme Court heard arguments for Gross's appeal on July 22, 2011, but the court rejected the appeal on August 5, 2011.

There had been some hope in April 2012 that Cuba would positively respond to a humanitarian request by Alan Gross to visit his elderly sick mother in the United States for a period of two weeks, but this did not occur. In contrast, a U.S. federal judge in Florida granted René González, one of the so-called "Cuban five" convicted in 2001, the right to visit his dying brother in Cuba for two weeks.

In September 2012, Judy Gross, the wife of Alan Gross, expressed concern in media reports about the health of her husband, who has lost more than 100 pounds while in prison, and fears that he would not survive continued imprisonment. In early October 2012, Judy Gross expressed concern that her husband could have cancer. In November 2012, the Cuban government maintained that Gross was in normal health and that a biopsy on a lesion showed that he did not have cancer.

In November 2012, Alan and Judy Gross filed a suit in U.S. District Court against the U.S. government and his employer, DAI, alleging that they "failed to disclose adequately to Mr. Gross, both before and after he began traveling to Cuba, the material risks that he faced due to his participation in the project."[109] DAI ultimately reached an undisclosed settlement with Alan and Judy Gross on May 16, 2013, while on May 28, 2013, a U.S. federal judge dismissed the lawsuit against the U.S. government. Gross's lawyers reportedly will appeal the judge's dismal.

---

[107] U.S. Department of State, Daily Press Briefing, May 11, 2012, available at http://www.state.gov/r/pa/prs/dpb/2012/05/189753.htm.

[108] Development Alternatives Inc. "Updated Statement from DAI President and CEO Dr. James Boomgard Regarding Detainee in Cuba," January 7, 2010, available at http://dai.com/news-publications/news/updated-statement-dai-president-and-ceo-dr-james-boomgard-regarding-detainee.

[109] David Adams, "American Contractor Jailed in Cuba Sues U.S., Employer for $60 Million," *Reuters*, November 16, 2012.

In the more than four years since Gross has been imprisoned, numerous U.S. officials and Members of Congress have raised the issue of Alan Gross's detention with the Cuban government and have called for his release. In late November 2012, Judy Gross urged President Obama to give the case top priority and to designate a special envoy to meet with the Cuban government for her husband's release.[110] On December 3, 2012, the third anniversary of Gross's imprisonment, the State Department issued a statement again calling for his release, and asked the Cuban government to grant Gross's request to travel to the United States to visit his gravely ill 90-year-old mother. On December 5, 2012, the Senate approved S.Res. 609 (Moran) by voice vote, marking the first congressional vote on the issue since Gross's detention. With 31 cosponsors, the resolution called for the immediate and unconditional release of Gross, and urged the Cuban government in the meantime to provide all appropriate diagnostic and medical treatment to address the full range of medical issues facing Mr. Gross and to allow him to choose a doctor to provide him with an independent medical assessment.

Cuban officials have called for talks with the United States aimed at resolving the Alan Gross case and continued to link his release to the case of the "Cuban five." In late May 2013, a high ranking Cuban foreign ministry official, Josefina Vidal, director for North American Affairs, met in Washington DC, with State Department official Roberta Jacobson, Assistant Secretary for Western Hemisphere Affairs, to discuss bilateral issues, including the Gross case. In August 2013, Cuba allowed a U.S. doctor to visit and examine Gross. As noted above, since 2012, Gross's lawyer had been calling for an independent medical examination by a doctor of Gross's choosing.[111]

The State Department maintains that securing the release of Alan Gross remains a top U.S. priority. The State Department maintains that it has been using every appropriate diplomatic channel to press for his release. On December 3, 2013, the fourth anniversary of his imprisonment, the State Department maintained that it was using every appropriate diplomatic channel, both publicly and privately, to press for Gross's release. The State Department also reiterated its call for the Cuban government to release Gross immediately, as did National Security Adviser Susan Rice.[112] Gross's incarceration has been raised by the United States at semi-annual migration talks with Cuba, including most recently on January 9, 2014. On January 14, 2014, in a meeting with the Vatican, Secretary of State Kerry asked for their assistance in securing the release of Gross.[113] The State Department issued a press statement on May 2, 1014, Gross's 65th birthday, expressing deep concern about his well-being and again calling on the Cuban government to release him and allow him to be reunited with his family. The statement also asserted that Gross's "detention remains an impediment to more constructive relations between Cuba and the United States."[114]

In early April 2014, Gross went on an nine-day hunger strike in which he was protesting his treatment by the Cuban and U.S. governments. He maintained that there would be further protests to come, and that his 91-year old mother had urged him to resume eating.[115] Later in April, Gross's lawyer, Scott Gilbert, maintained that his client planned to return from Cuba to his family

---

[110] "Judy Gross Urges Action from Obama to Get Husband Released," *EFE News Service,* November 30, 2012.

[111] "Cuba Says Imprisoned American in "Normal" Health," *Agence France Presse*, November 28, 2012.

[112] U.S. Department of State, Daily Press Briefing, December 3, 2013.

[113] Warren Strobel, "Kerry Asks Vatican to Help Win Release of American Jailed in Cuba," *Reuters*, January 14, 2014.

[114] U.S. Department of State, "Continued Detention of Alan Gross," Press Statement, May 2, 2014.

[115] "U.S. Government Contractor Jailed in Cuba Ends Hunger Strike," *Reuters*, April 11, 2014.

---

within the year, and that his 65th birthday in Cuba—on May 2, 2014—would be his last because he would renew a hunger strike if he is not released within the year. Gilbert maintains that Gross's imprisonment has taken a toll on his health, with some lost vision in his right eye, a missing tooth, a limp because of his hips, and weight loss of nearly 110 pounds. He maintained that Cuban Foreign Minister Bruno Rodriguez has reiterated Cuba's "strong interest in sitting down with officials of the United States at the highest levels to resolve this issue with no preconditions."[116]

Radio and TV Marti

U.S.-government sponsored radio and television broadcasting to Cuba—Radio and TV Martí—began in 1985 and 1990 respectively. According to the *Broadcasting Board of Governors (BBG) FY2015 Congressional Budget Request*, Radio and TV Martí "inform and engage the people of Cuba by providing a reliable and credible source of news and information." The BBG's Office of Cuba Broadcasting uses "a mix of media, including shortwave, medium wave, direct-to-home satellite, Internet, flash drives, and DVDs to help reach audiences in Cuba."[117]

Until October 1999, U.S.-government funded international broadcasting programs had been a primary function of the United States Information Agency (USIA). When USIA was abolished and its functions were merged into the Department of State at the beginning of FY2000, the BBG became an independent agency that included such entities as the Voice of America (VOA), Radio Free Europe/Radio Liberty (RFE/RL), Radio Free Asia, and the Office of Cuba Broadcasting (OCB), which manages Radio and TV Marti. OCB is headquartered in Miami, FL. Legislation in the 104th Congress (P.L. 104-134) required the relocation of OCB from Washington, DC, to South Florida. The move began in 1996 and was completed in 1998.

TV Martí programming has been broadcast through multiple transmission methods over the years. Its broadcasts are transmitted via the Internet and satellite television 24 hours a day, seven days per week. From its beginning in 1990 until July 2005, TV Martí was broadcast via an aerostat (blimp) from facilities in Cudjoe Key, FL, for four and one-half hours daily, but the aerostat was destroyed by Hurricane Dennis. From mid-2004 until 2006, TV Martí programming was transmitted for several hours once a week via an airborne platform known as Commando Solo operated by the Department of Defense utilizing a C-130 aircraft. In August 2006, OCB began to use contracted private aircraft to transmit prerecorded TV Martí broadcasts, and by late October 2006 the OCB inaugurated an aircraft-broadcasting platform known as AeroMartí with the capability of transmitting live broadcasts. In recent years, AeroMartí transmitted broadcasts two and one-half hours for five days weekly, but beginning in May 2013, AeroMartí flights were curtailed because of the FY2013 budget sequestration.[118] Moreover, as noted below, the BBG proposed eliminating AeroMartí in its FY2013 and FY2014 budget requests because of decreases in its cost effectiveness, and it was ultimately eliminated in FY2014.

According to the BBG, the OCB uses multiple web domains and anti-censorship tools such as web-based proxies to reach Internet users in Cuba. Since 2011, the OCB has used SMS

---

[116] Marc Frank, "Jailed U.S. Contractor in Cuba Warns of Terminal Hunger Strike," *Reuters*, April 23, 2014.

[117] See the full text of the Broadcasting Board of Governors FY2015 budget request, available at http://www.bbg.gov/wp-content/media/2014/03/FY-2015-BBG-Congressional-Budget-Request-FINAL-21-March-2014.pdf.

[118] David A. Fahrenthold, "Grounded: TV Martí Plane a Monument to the Limits of American Austerity.

messaging to communicate with audiences in Cuba, allowing OCB to "push" information to mobile phone users in Cuba in a manner that is difficult to filter. The OCB's website, martinoticias.com, began streaming Radio and TV Martí programming 24 hours a day in 2013. It has also launched a YouTube Channel, Facebook page, and Twitter feed.

Funding for Cuba Broadcasting

From FY1984 through FY2013, Congress appropriated about $745 million for broadcasting to Cuba. In recent years, funding amounted to $28.416 million in FY2011, $27.977 million in FY2012, and an estimated $28.266 million in FY2013 (not including sequestration reductions). The FY2014 request was for $23.804 million, and Congress ultimately appropriated $27.043 million.

FY2012. The Administration requested $28.475 million for Cuba broadcasting in FY2012. The Senate Appropriations Committee version of the FY2012 State Department, Foreign Operations, and Related Programs Appropriations measure, S. 1601 (S.Rept. 112-85), recommended $28.181 million in funding for Cuba broadcasting, $294,000 less than the request. In contrast, a draft House Appropriations Committee report and bill (marked up by the House Appropriations Committee's Subcommittee on State, Foreign Operations, and Related Programs on July 27, 2011) recommended $30.175 million for Cuba broadcasting, $1.7 million more than the request. (See the draft committee report, available at http://appropriations.house.gov/UploadedFiles/ FY12-SFOPSCombinedReport-CSBA.pdf.) In final action on the FY2012 Consolidated Appropriations Act (H.R. 2055, P.L. 112-74), Congress approved full funding of the Administration's $28.475 million request for broadcasting to Cuba. The BBG's actual spending for FY2012 funding was $27.977 million.

FY2013. The Administration requested $23.594 million for Cuba broadcasting in FY2013, almost $4.5 million lower than FY2012 funding. According to the BBG's budget request, program reductions are possible because of OCB's planned streamlining in the planning and execution of news coverage and reliance on additional technical support from the BBG's International Broadcasting Bureau. The BBG proposed eliminating the AeroMartí platform for a savings of $2 million because of decreases in its cost effectiveness.

The Senate Appropriations Committee-reported FY2013 State Department, Foreign Operations, and Related Programs Appropriations Act, S. 3241 (S.Rept. 112-172), would have provided $23.4 million ($194,000 less than the Administration's request). The committee's report to the bill expressed its support for "the proposed reduction in TV Martí operating costs, including the termination of the Aeromartí contract, as long as such action will not reduce its current broadcast schedule of 166 weekly hours." The House Appropriations Committee-reported bill, H.R. 5857 (H.Rept. 112-494), would have provided $28.062 million ($4.468 million more than the Administration's request and the same amount provided in FY2012).

As already noted, Congress did not complete action on FY2013 appropriations before the end of the fiscal year, but in September 2012 it approved a continuing resolution (P.L. 112-175) that continued funding through March 27, 2013, at the same rate for projects and activities in FY2012 plus an across-the-board increase of 0.612%. On March 21, 2013, Congress completed action on FY2013 appropriations with the approval of H.R. 933 (P.L. 113-6), but it did not stop funding reductions caused by sequestration set forth in the Budget Control Act of 2011 (P.L. 112-25), as amended by the American Taxpayer Relief Act (P.L. 112-240). In its FY2014 Congressional

Budget Request, the BBG maintained that the FY2013 enacted level for Cuba broadcasting was $28.266 million, but this did not reflect the funding reduction caused by sequestration. In May 2013, because of sequestration, the OCB curtailed AeroMartí flights that transmitted TV Martí broadcasts.

FY2014. The Administration requested $23.804 million for Cuba broadcasting, about $4.5 million less than that provided in FY2013, although roughly similar to the FY2013 budget request for Cuba broadcasting. In terms of program reductions, the BBG again proposed eliminating AeroMartí an aircraft-based broadcast system targeting Havana and surrounding areas, because of decreases in cost effectiveness. The BBG maintains that the signal is heavily jammed by the Cuban government, significantly limiting its reach and impact in Cuba. (As noted above, the OCB curtailed AeroMartí flights beginning in May 2013 because of the FY2013 budget sequestration.) The OCB would also eliminate the use of two shortwave frequencies at night. The BBG is also proposing to eliminate seven OCB positions working in a unit that served as a clearinghouse for research and information on issues related to Cuba. It is also proposing to reduce contractors and up to 50 OCB positions. According to the BBG's budget request, the agency will seek to execute inter-agency agreements with the Department of State and the U.S. Agency for International Development to utilize some existing unobligated resources allocated for Cuba democracy, human rights, and entrepreneurship programs; the BBG would use the resources to fund OCB's special TV programming and to maintain a 24 hours per day broadcast schedule.

The House Appropriations Committee version of the FY2014 Department of State, Foreign Operations, and Related Programs Appropriations Act, H.R. 2855 (H.Rept. 113-185, reported July 30, 2013), would have provided $28.266 million for Cuba broadcasting, about $4.5 million more than the Administration's request. In contrast, the Senate Appropriations Committee version, S. 1372 (S.Rept. 113-81, reported July 25, 2013), would have provided $23.804 million, the same amount as the Administration's request.

Congress ultimately appropriated $27.043 million for Cuba broadcasting when it enacted the FY2014 omnibus appropriations measure, H.R. 3547 (P.L. 113-76), signed into law January 17, 2014. This amounted to about $3.24 million above the Administration's request.

Oversight of Radio and TV Martí

Both Radio and TV Martí have at times been the focus of controversies, including questions about adherence to broadcast standards. There have been various attempts over the years to cut funding for the programs, especially for TV Martí, which has not had much of an audience because of Cuban jamming efforts. From 1990 through 2008, there were numerous government studies and audits of the OCB, including investigations by the GAO, by a 1994 congressionally established Advisory Panel on Radio and TV Martí, by the State Department Office Inspector General (OIG), and by the combined State Department/BBG Office Inspector General.[119]

---

[119] See the following reports and audits from 1990 through 2008: U.S. General Accounting Office (GAO), *Broadcasts to Cuba, TV Marti Surveys are Flawed*, GAO/NSIAD-90-252, August 1990; U.S. GAO, *TV Marti, Costs and Compliance with Broadcast Standards and International Agreements*, GAO/NSIAD-92-199, May 1992; U.S. GAO, Letter to Hon. Howard L. Berman and Hon. John F. Kerry regarding Radio Marti broadcast standards, GAO/NSIAD-93-126R, February 17, 1993; Advisory Panel on Radio and TV Marti, *Report of the Advisory Panel on Radio and TV Marti*, Three Volumes, March 1994; U.S. GAO, *Radio Marti, Program Review Processes Need Strengthening*, (continued...)

In January 2009, GAO issued a report asserting that the best available research suggests that Radio and TV Martí's audience is small, and cited telephone surveys since 2003 showing that less than 2% of respondents reported tuning in to Radio or TV Martí during the past week. With regard to TV Martí viewership, according to the report, all of the IBB's telephone surveys since 2003 show that less than 1% of respondents said that they had watched TV Martí during the past week. According to the GAO report, the IBB surveys show that there was no increase in reported TV Martí viewership following the beginning of AeroMartí and DirecTV satellite broadcasting in 2006. The GAO report also cited concerns with adherence to relevant domestic laws and international standards, including the domestic dissemination of OCB programming, inappropriate advertisements during OCB programming, and TV Martí's interference with Cuban broadcasts.[120] GAO testified on its report in a hearing held by the House Subcommittee on International Organizations, Human Rights, and Oversight of the Committee on Foreign Affairs on June 17, 2009.

In April 2010, the Senate Foreign Relations Committee majority issued a staff report that concluded that Radio and TV Martí "continue to fail in their efforts to influence Cuban society, politics, and policy." The report cited problems with adherence to broadcast standards, audience size, and Cuban government jamming. Among its recommendations, the report called for the IBB to move the Office of Cuba Broadcasting back to Washington and integrate it fully into the Voice of America.[121]

In December 2011, GAO issued a report examining the extent to which the BBG's strategic plan for broadcasting required by the conference report to the FY2010 Consolidated Appropriations measure (H.Rept. 111-366 to H.R. 3288/P.L. 111-117) met the requirements established in the legislation. The BBG strategic plan was required to include (1) an analysis of the current situation in Cuba and an allocation of resources consistent with the relative priority of broadcasting to Cuba as determined by the annual Language Service Review and other factors; (2) the estimated audience sizes in Cuba for Radio and TV Martí and the sources and relative reliability of the data; (3) the cost of any and all types of TV transmission and the effectiveness of each in increasing such audience size; (4) the principal obstacles to increasing audience size; (5) an analysis of other options for disseminating news and information to Cuba and the cost effectiveness of each option; and (6) an analysis of the program efficiencies and effectiveness that can be achieved through shared resources and cost saving opportunities in radio and television production between Radio and TV Martí and the Voice of America. GAO found that the BBG's strategic plan lacked key information. Of the six requirements set forth in the conference report, the GAO found that the

---

(...continued)

GAO/NSIAD-94-265, September 1994; U.S. GAO, *U.S. Information Agency, Issues Related to Reinvention Planning in the Office of Cuba Broadcasting*, GAO/NSIAD-96-110, May 1996; U.S. Department of State, Office of the Inspector General, *Review of Policies and Procedures for Ensuring that Radio Marti Broadcasts Adhere to Applicable Requirements*, 99-IB-010, June 1999; U.S. Department of State and the Broadcasting Board of Governors, Office of Inspector General, *Review of the Effectiveness and Implementation of Office of Cuba Broadcasting's New Program Initiatives*, Report No. IBO-A-03-01, January 2003, and *Report of Inspection, Office of Cuba Broadcasting*, Report No. ISP-IB 07-35, June 2007; and U.S. GAO, *Broadcasting to Cuba, Weaknesses in Contracting Practices Reduced Visibility into Selected Award Decisions*, GAO-08-764, July 2008.

[120] U.S. GAO, *Broadcasting to Cuba, Actions Are Needed to Improve Strategy and Operations*, GAO-09-127, January 2009.

[121] U.S. Congress, Senate Committee on Foreign Relations, *Cuba: Immediate Action Is Needed To Ensure the Survivability of Radio and TV Marti*, committee print, 111th Cong., 2nd sess., April 29, 2010, S.Prt. 111-46 (Washington: GPO, 2010).

BBG's strategic plan fully addressed item (4) regarding the principal obstacles to increasing audience sized, but only partially addressed the other five items. The GAO report stated that the BBG can develop and provide more information to Congress, including an analysis of the cost savings opportunities of sharing resources between Radio and TV Martí and the Voice of America's Latin America Division.[122]

In May 2012, a controversy occurred involving an editorial by OCB Director Carlos García-Pérez in which he strongly criticized Cuban Cardinal Jaime Ortega and referred to the Cardinal as a "lackey" of the Cuban government.[123] The strong language was criticized by several Members of Congress, who called for the Administration to reject the comments against Cardinal Ortega.[124] The editorial raised significant questions about the editorial policy of OCB as well as OCB's adherence to broadcast standards.[125] Such an editorial, authored by the director of OCB, could lead one to conclude that the views articulated were those of the U.S. government. BBG's Director of Communications and External Affairs Lynne Weil maintained that such "editorials, unless otherwise stated, represent the views of the broadcasters only and not necessarily those of the U.S. government."[126]

Terrorism Issues[127]

Cuba was added to the State Department's list of states sponsoring international terrorism in 1982 (pursuant to Section 6(j) of the Export Administration Act of 1979; P.L. 96-72; 50 U.S.C. Appendix 2504(j)) because of its alleged ties to international terrorism and support for terrorist groups in Latin America, and it has remained on the list since that time. Cuba had a long history of supporting revolutionary movements and governments in Latin America and Africa, but in 1992, Fidel Castro said that his country's support for insurgents abroad was a thing of the past. Cuba's change in policy was in large part due to the breakup of the Soviet Union, which resulted in the loss of billions of dollars in annual subsidies to Cuba, and led to substantial Cuban economic decline.

Critics of retaining Cuba on the terrorism list maintain that it is a holdover from the Cold War. They argue that domestic political considerations keep Cuba on the terrorism list and maintain that Cuba's presence on the list diverts U.S. attention from struggles against serious terrorist threats. Those who support keeping Cuba on the terrorism list argue that there is ample evidence that Cuba supports terrorism. They point to the government's history of supporting terrorist acts

---

[122] U.S. Government Accountability Office, *Broadcasting Board of Governors Should Provide Additional Information to Congress Regarding Broadcasting to Cuba*, December 13, 2011, available at http://www.gao.gov/assets/590/586869.pdf.

[123] William Booth, "U.S. Broadcaster Call Archbishop a Castro "Lackey," Washington Post, May 6, 2012. The editorial no longer appears on the website of Radio/TV Martí, but is available at http://porcubaparacuba.blogspot.com/2012/05/editorial-de-radio-y-tv-marti-acerca.html.

[124] See a letter to Secretary of State Hillary Rodham Clinton, a member of the Broadcasting Board of Governors, from five Members of Congress, May 8, 2012, available at http://www.democracyinamericas.org/pdfs/ortegaletter.pdf.

[125] Authorization legislation establishing both Radio and TV Martí require broadcasting to Cuba to be in accordance with all Voice of America standards to ensure the broadcast of programs which are objective, accurate, balanced, and which present a variety of views (§3(b) of P.L. 98-111, as amended, and §243(b) of P.L. 101-246, as amended).

[126] William Booth, "U.S. Broadcaster Calls Archbishop a Castro "Lackey," *Washington Post*, May 6, 2012.

[127] For background information, see archived CRS Report RL32251, *Cuba and the State Sponsors of Terrorism List*, by Mark P. Sullivan, August 22, 2006.

and armed insurgencies in Latin America and Africa. They point to the government's continued hosting of members of foreign terrorist organizations and U.S. fugitives from justice.

In its *Country Reports on Terrorism 2013* report (issued April 30, 2014), the State Department stated that Cuba has long provided safe have to members of the Basque Fatherland and Liberty (ETA) and the Revolutionary Armed Forces of Colombia (FARC). The report noted, however, that Cuba's ties to ETA have become more distant and that about eight of the two dozen ETA members in Cuba were relocated with the cooperation of the Spanish government. With regard to the FARC, the terrorism report noted that throughout 2012, the Cuban government supported and hosted peace negotiations between the FARC and the Colombian government. As in its 2011 and 2012 reports, the State Department stated in the 2013 terrorism report that "there was no indication that the Cuban government provided weapons or paramilitary training to terrorist groups."[128]

Another issue noted in the 2013 terrorism report that has been mentioned for many years in the annual report is Cuba's harboring of fugitives wanted in the United States. The report maintained that Cuba provided such support as housing, food ration books, and medical care for these individuals. U.S. fugitives from justice in Cuba include convicted murderers and numerous hijackers, most of whom entered Cuba in the 1970s and early 1980s.[129] For example, Joanne Chesimard, also known as Assata Shakur, was added to the FBI's Most Wanted Terrorist list on May 2, 2013. Chesimard was part of militant group known as the Black Liberation Army. In 1977, she was convicted for the 1973 murder of a New Jersey State Police officer and sentenced to life in prison. Chesimard escaped from prison in 1979, and according to the FBI, lived underground before fleeing to Cuba in 1984.[130] In addition to Chesimard and other fugitives from the past, a number of U.S. fugitives from justice wanted for Medicare and other types of insurance fraud reportedly have fled to Cuba in recent years.[131] On November 6, 2013, William Potts, an American citizen who had hijacked an airplane from New Jersey to Havana in 1984, returned to the United States to face air-piracy charges; he had served 14 years in a Cuban jail for his crime. In the 113th Congress, H.Res. 262 (King, NY), introduced in June 2013, calls for the immediate extradition or rendering of convicted felon William Morales and all other fugitives from justice who are receiving safe harbor in Cuba in order to escape prosecution or confinement for criminal offenses committed in the United States.

Cuba in recent years has returned wanted fugitives to the United States on a case by case basis. For example, in 2011, U.S. Marshals picked up a husband and wife in Cuba who were wanted for a 2010 murder in New Jersey,[132] while in April 2013, Cuba returned a Florida couple who had allegedly kidnapped their own children (who had been in the custody of the mother's parents) and fled to Havana.[133] However, Cuba has generally refused to render to U.S. justice any fugitive

---

[128] U.S. Department of State, *Country Reports on Terrorism 2013*, April 30, 2014.

[129] U.S. Department of State, *Country Reports on Terrorism 2007*, April 30, 2008.

[130] FBI, Most Wanted Terrorists, Joanne Deborah Chesimard, Poster, at http://www.fbi.gov/wanted/wanted_terrorists/joanne-deborah-chesimard/view.

[131] For example, see The United States Attorney's Office, Southern District of Florida, "Thirty-three Defendants Charged in Staged Automobile Accident Scheme," Press Release, May 16, 201; Legal Forum, Experts: Florida Couple May Not Be Welcome in Cuba," *Naples Daily News*, April 9, 2013; and Jay Weaver, "FBI Struggling to Catch Dozens of Fraud Fugitives Hiding in Cuba," *Miami Herald*, July 16, 2011.

[132] George Mast, "Murder Suspects Caught in Cuba," *Courier-Post* (New Jersey), September 30, 2011.

[133] Paul Haven and Peter Orsi, "Cuba Says It Will Give U.S. Florida Couple Who Allegedly Kidnapped Children," *Associated Press*, April 9, 2013.

---

judged by Cuba to be "political," such as Chesimard, who they believe could not receive a fair trial in the United States. Moreover, Cuba in the past has responded to U.S. extradition requests by stating that approval would be contingent upon the United States returning wanted Cuban criminals from the United States. These include the return of Luis Posada Carriles, whom Cuba accused of plotting the 1976 bombing of a Cuban jet that killed 73 people.[134] Cuba had also long sought the return of a militant Cuban exile, Orlando Bosch, whom Cuba also accused of responsibility for the 1976 airplane bombing (Bosch died in Florida in 2011).

The 2012 terrorism report, issued in May 2013, had noted that Cuba became a member of the Financial Action Task Force of South America (GAFISUD), a regional group associated with the multilateral Financial Action Task Force (FATF), in December 2012. As such, Cuba has committed to adopting and implementing the 40 recommendations of the FATF pertaining to international standards on combating money laundering and the financing of terrorism and proliferation.[135] Cuba is scheduled to undergo a GAFISUD mutual evaluation in 2014 examining its compliance and implementation of the FATF recommendations.[136]

As set forth in Section 6(j) of the Export Administration Act, a country's retention on the state sponsors of terrorism list may be rescinded by the President in two ways. The first option is for the President to submit a report to Congress certifying that there has been a fundamental change in the leadership and policies of the government and that the government is not supporting acts of international terrorism and is providing assurances that it will not support such acts in the future. The second option is for the President to submit a report to Congress, at least 45 days in advance justifying the rescission and certifying that the government has not provided any support for international terrorism during the preceding six-months, and has provided assurances that it will not support such acts in the future.

Another potential option to remove Cuba from the state sponsors of terrorism list is set forth in H.R. 1917 (Rush) introduced in the 113th Congress. Section 10 of the bill would rescind any determination of the Secretary of State in effect on the date of enactment of the Act that Cuba has repeatedly provided support for acts of international terrorism. The bill referenced not only Section 6(j) of the Export Administration Act (50 U.S.C. Appendix 2504(j)), but also Section 620A of the Foreign Assistance Act of 1961(22 U.S.C. 2371) and Section 40 of the Arms Export Control Act (22 U.S.C. 2780).

A press report in February 2013 claimed that high ranking State Department officials concluded that Cuba should not be on the state sponsors of terrorism list, but State Department officials contend that the report was incorrect and that there are no current plans to remove Cuba from the list.[137] The State Department conducts an annual review to see whether a country should be on the list. Some observers maintain that Cuba's role in facilitating Colombia's peace talks could ultimately be a factor in removing Cuba from the list.

---

[134] For more background on Posada, see CRS Report RS21049, *Latin America: Terrorism Issues*.

[135] Financial Action Task Force, International Standards on Combating Money Laundering and the Financing of Terrorism & Proliferation, The FATF Recommendations," February 2012, available at http://www.gafisud.info/documentos/eng/40_Recommendations.pdf.

[136] See the website of the GAFISUD at http://www.gafisud.info/eng-index.php.

[137] Bryan Bender, "Talk Grows of Taking Cuba Off Terror List," *Boston Globe*, February 21, 2013; U.S. Department of State, Daily Press Briefing, February 21, 2013.

Migration Issues[138]

Cuba and the United States reached two migration accords in 1994 and 1995 designed to stem the mass exodus of Cubans attempting to reach the United States by boat. On the minds of U.S. policy makers was the 1980 Mariel boatlift in which 125,000 Cubans fled to the United States with the approval of Cuban officials. In response to Fidel Castro's threat to unleash another Mariel, U.S. officials reiterated U.S. resolve not to allow another exodus. Amid escalating numbers of fleeing Cubans, on August 19, 1994, President Clinton abruptly changed U.S. migration policy, under which Cubans attempting to flee their homeland were allowed into the United States, and announced that the U.S. Coast Guard and Navy would take Cubans rescued at sea to the U.S. naval base at Guantanamo Bay, Cuba. Despite the change in policy, Cubans continued fleeing in large numbers.

As a result, in early September 1994, Cuba and the United States began talks that culminated in a September 9, 1994, bilateral agreement to stem the flow of Cubans fleeing to the United States by boat. In the agreement, the United States and Cuba agreed to facilitate safe, legal, and orderly Cuban migration to the United States, consistent with a 1984 migration agreement. The United States agreed to ensure that total legal Cuban migration to the United States would be a minimum of 20,000 each year, not including immediate relatives of U.S. citizens.

In May 1995, the United States reached another accord with Cuba under which the United States would parole the more than 30,000 Cubans housed at Guantanamo into the United States, but would intercept future Cuban migrants attempting to enter the United States by sea and would return them to Cuba. The two countries would cooperate jointly in the effort. Both countries also pledged to ensure that no action would be taken against those migrants returned to Cuba as a consequence of their attempt to immigrate illegally. On January 31, 1996, the Department of Defense announced that the last of some 32,000 Cubans intercepted at sea and housed at Guantanamo had left the U.S. Naval Station, most having been paroled into the United States.

Since the 1995 migration accord, the U.S. Coast Guard has interdicted thousands of Cubans at sea and returned them to their country. Those Cubans who reach shore are allowed to apply for permanent resident status in one year, pursuant to the Cuban Adjustment Act of 1966 (P.L. 89-732). In short, most interdictions, even in U.S. coastal waters, result in a return to Cuba, while those Cubans who touch shore are allowed to stay in the United States. This so-called "wet foot/dry foot" policy has been criticized by some as encouraging Cubans to risk their lives in order to make it to the United States and as encouraging alien smuggling. Others maintain that U.S. policy should welcome those migrants fleeing communist Cuba whether or not they are able to make it to land.

The number of Cubans interdicted at sea by the U.S. Coast Guard rose from 666 in FY2002 to a high of 2,868 in FY2007. In the three subsequent years, maritime interdictions declined significantly to 422 by FY2010 (see **Figure 6**). Major reasons for the decline were reported to include the U.S. economic downturn, more efficient coastal patrolling, and more aggressive prosecution of migrant smugglers by both the United States and Cuba.[139]

---

[138] For additional background on migration issues through mid-2009, see CRS Report R40566, *Cuban Migration to the United States: Policy and Trends*, by Ruth Ellen Wasem.

[139] Alfonso Chardy and Juan Tamayo, "Exodus of Cubans Slowing," *Miami Herald*, October 6, 2010.

From FY2011-FY2013, however, the number of Cubans interdicted by the Coast Guard increased each year, from 985 in FY2011 to 1,357 in FY2013. In FY2014, some 890 Cuban migrants were interdicted as of May 7, 2014.[140] Speculation on the reasons for the increase include Cuba's poor economic and political situation; the Coast Guard's more efficient methods of interdiction; and the easing of the economic situation in the United States, making it easier for the payment of fees to migrant smugglers.[141]

Figure 6. Maritime Interdictions of Cubans by the U.S. Coast Guard, FY2002-FY2014

As of May 7, 2014

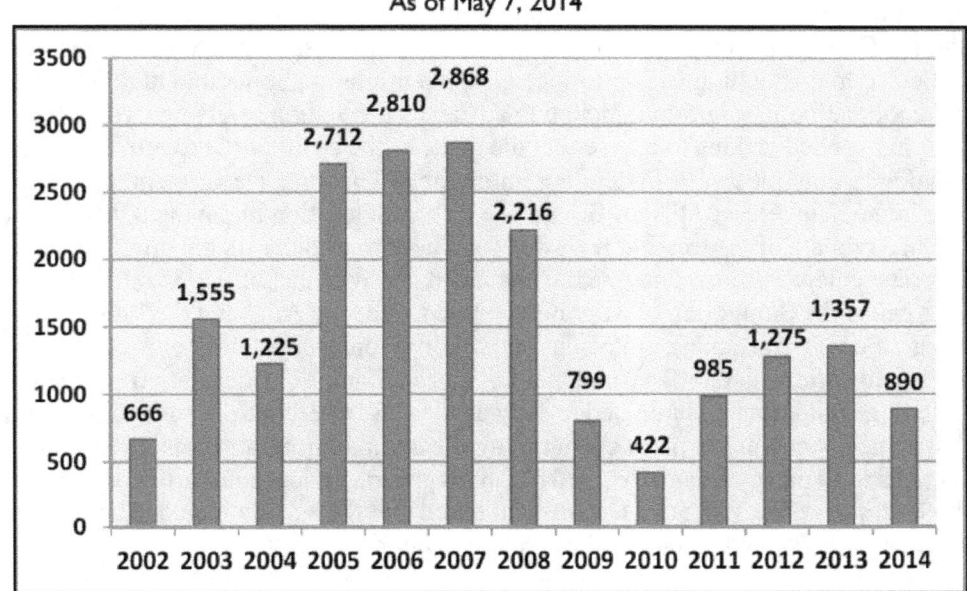

Source: Created by CRS using information provided by the United States Coast Guard, Alien Migrant Interdiction, "Total Interdictions – Fiscal Year 1982 to Present," January 8, 2014, current statistics available at http://www.uscg.mil/hq/cg5/cg531/AMIO/FlowStats/FY.asp.

Despite the U.S. Coast Guard's maritime interdiction program, thousands of unauthorized Cubans reach the United States each year, either by boat or, especially, at land ports of entry. U.S. Border Patrol apprehensions between ports of entry (largely coastal Florida) of unauthorized Cubans were 910 in FY2009, 712 in FY2010, 959 in FY2011, and 606 in FY2012. These statistics are significantly lower than the FY2005-FY2008 period when Border Patrol apprehensions of Cubans averaged over 3,700 each year.[142] According to the State Department, Cubans continue to favor land-based entry at U.S. ports of entry, especially from Mexico. In FY2012, 11,106 Cubans presented themselves at land border ports of entry, while in FY2013, that figure rose to 13,764

---

[140] U.S. Coast Guard, Alien Migrant Interdiction, Coast Guard Office of Law Enforcement, "Total Interdictions, Fiscal Year 1982 to Present," January 8, 2014.

[141] Alfonso Chardy and Juan O. Tamayo, "Illegal Cuban Migration, After Years of Decline, Is Up Again," Miami Herald, *Miami Herald*, October 8, 2011; Alfonso Chardy and Juan O. Tamayo, "Number of Cubans Trying to Enter U.S. Increases," *Miami Herald*, June 17, 2012.

[142] U.S. Department of Homeland Security, Office of Immigration Statistics, "Apprehensions by the U.S. Border Patrol: 2005-2010," July 2011; FY2011 and FY2012 statistics provided to CRS by U.S. Border Patrol.

Cubans.[143] (In October 2008, Mexico and Cuba negotiated a migration accord in an attempt to curb the irregular flow of migrants through Mexico.)[144]

Semi-annual U.S.-Cuban talks alternating between Cuba and the United States were held on the implementation of the 1994/1995 migration accords until they were suspended by the United States in 2004. The Obama Administration re-started the talks in 2009, and there were four rounds of talks until January 2011. In addition to migration issues, the talks became a forum to raise other issues of concern, including, for U.S. officials, the imprisonment of Alan Gross.

After an 18-month hiatus, another round of migration talks was held on July 17, 2013 in Washington, DC. After the talks, the State Department issued a statement maintaining that the agenda reflected long-standing U.S. priorities on Cuba migration issues and highlighted areas of successful cooperation in migration, including advances in aviation safety and visa processing and identifying needed actions to ensure that the goals of the accord are fully met, especially with regard to safeguarding the lives of intending immigrants. The State Department also reiterated the call for the immediate release of Alan Gross. The Cuban delegation maintained that the meeting took place in a climate of respect and reviewed joint actions to deter illegal migration and alien smuggling. The delegation also noted that Cuba had recently (June 20, 2013) ratified the "Protocol Against the Smuggling of Migrants by Land, Sea, and Air," and the Protocol to Prevent, Suppress, and Punish Trafficking in Persons, especially Women and Children," both supplements to the U.N. Convention against Transnational Organized Crime. The delegation also said that alien smuggling could not be eliminated as long as the U.S. "wet foot/dry foot policy" and the Cuban Adjustment Act were in place encouraging illegal immigration. Another round of migration talks took place on January 9, 2014, and both sides issued similarly positive statements noting the issues covered. The State Department noted that the agenda included cooperation on aviation security, search and rescue, and consular document fraud.[145]

On two occasions since late 2013, Cuba has suspended its consular services (e.g., passports, passport renewals, visas) in the United States because it has not been able to find a replacement financial institution to replace M&T Bank, which had decided to stop offering bank services to Cuba's diplomatic missions. According to press reports, the State Department has maintained that it has been working with Cuba to help resolve the issue. The first suspension of services began November 26, 2013, but the services were restored on December 9 after M&T Bank postponed closing the accounts of its diplomatic missions in Washington, DC, and New York until March 1, 2014. The second suspension of services began on February 14, 2014, but Cuba's diplomatic missions in the United States reportedly had again resumed all consular services, although Cuba had reportedly still not found a bank to replace M&T.[146]

---

[143] U.S. Department of State, "Cuban Compliance with the Migration Accords, (April 2013 to October 2013)," Report to Congress, October 22, 2013.

[144] Diego Cevallos, "Migration: More and More Cubans Entering U.S. Through Mexico," *Inter Press Service News Agency*, June 17, 2008.

[145] U.S. Department of State, "Migration Talks with Cuba," January 10, 2014; Republic of Cuba, Ministry of Foreign Affairs, "Press Release Issued by the Cuban delegation to the Round of Migration Talks with the United States," January 9, 2014.

[146] U.S. Department of State, "Migration Talks with Cuba," January 10, 2014; Republic of Cuba, Ministry of Foreign Affairs, "Press Release Issued by the Cuban delegation to the Round of Migration Talks with the United States," January 9, 2014; and Juan O. Tamayo, "Cuba Resumes Processing All Consular Affairs," *Miami Herald*, May 15, 2014.

Cuba Alters Its Policy Regarding Exit Permits

In October 2012, the Cuban government announced that it would be updating its migration policy, effective January 14, 2013, by eliminating the long-standing policy of requiring an exit permit and letter of invitation from abroad for Cubans to travel abroad. Cubans are now able to travel abroad with just an updated passport and a visa issued by the country of destination, if required. Under the change in policy, Cubans can travel abroad for up to two years without forgoing their rights as Cuban citizens. The practice of requiring an exit permit had been extremely unpopular in Cuba and the government had been considering doing away with the practice for some time.

The Cuban government said that it would fight against "brain drain," and that the new policy would not apply to scientists, athletes, and other professionals. In early January 2013, however, the Cuban government announced that the new travel policy would also apply to health care professionals, including doctors.

When the new policy went into effect on January 14, 2013, thousands of Cubans lined up at government migration offices and travel agencies. Travel under the new policy requires an updated passport as well as any visas required by the receiving countries. While most countries require visas for Cubans, several Caribbean countries do not. Ecuador, which had not required a visa for Cubans visiting up to 90 days, announced on January 15, 2013, that it would require Cubans who wanted to visit to provide a letter of invitation from a legal resident in Ecuador with a commitment to cover expenses for the visiting Cuban(s).[147]

A U.S. State Department spokesman said that it welcomes any changes that would allow Cubans to depart from and return to their country freely. According to the State Department, Cuba's announced change is consistent with the Universal Declaration of Human Rights in that everyone should have the rights to leave any country, including their own, and return.[148]

As noted above, Internet blogger Yoani Sánchez and several other prominent dissidents and human rights activists have traveled abroad because of Cuba's new migration policy. In light of Cuba's new travel policy, some analysts have raised the question as to whether the United States should review its policy toward Cuban migrants, as set forth in the Cuban Adjustment Act of 1966 (P.L. 89-732), in which those Cubans arriving in the United States are allowed to apply for permanent resident status in one year.[149]

Effective August 1, 2013, the State Department made non-immigrant B-2 visas issued to Cubans for family visits, tourism, medical treatment, or other personal travel valid for five years with multiple entries. Previously these visas had been restricted to single entry for six months, and an extensive visa interview backlog had developed at the U.S. Interests Section in Havana. State

---

[147] Republic of Ecuador, Ministry of Foreign Relations, Commerce, and Integration, "Ecuador Requerirá Carta de Invitación par Ingreso de Ciudadanos Cubanos," Press Release, January 15, 2013.

[148] U.S. Department of State, "Daily Press Briefing," October 16, 2012.

[149] David Adams and Tom Brown, "Cuban Perks Under Scrutiny in U.S. Immigration Reform," *Reuters News*, February 8, 2013; Stephen Johnson "Recommendations for the New Administration: Interests, Policies, and Challenges in the Americas," Center for Strategic and International Studies, November 21, 2012; and Philip Peters, "Migration Policy Reform: Cuba Gets Started, U.S. Should Follow," Lexington Institute, December 2012.

Department officials maintain that the change increases people-to-people ties and removes procedural and financial burdens on Cuban travelers.[150]

Anti-Drug Cooperation

Cuba is not a major producer or consumer of illicit drugs, but its extensive shoreline and geographic location make it susceptible to narcotics smuggling operations. Drugs that enter the Cuban market are largely the result of onshore wash-ups from smuggling by high-speed boats moving drugs from Jamaica to the Bahamas, Haiti, and the United States or by small aircraft from clandestine airfields in Jamaica. For a number of years, Cuban officials have expressed concerns over the use of their waters and airspace for drug transit and about increased domestic drug use. The Cuban government has taken a number of measures to deal with the drug problem, including legislation to stiffen penalties for traffickers, increased training for counternarcotics personnel, and cooperation with a number of countries on anti-drug efforts.

According to the State Department's 2014 *International Narcotics Control Strategy Report (INCSR)*, issued February 28, 2014, Cuba has a number of anti-drug-related agreements in place with other countries, including 35 bilateral agreements for counterdrug cooperation and 27 policing cooperation agreements. Since 1999, Cuba's Operation Hatchet has focused on maritime and air interdiction and the recovery of narcotics washed up on Cuban shores. As reported in the *INCSR*, Cuba reported interdicting 3.05 metric tons of illegal narcotics in 2012, with the overwhelming majority consisting of wash ups. Since 2003, Cuba has aggressively pursued an internal enforcement and investigation program against its incipient drug market with an effective nationwide drug prevention and awareness campaign.

Over the years, there have been varying levels of U.S.-Cuban cooperation on anti-drug efforts. In 1996, Cuban authorities cooperated with the United States in the seizure of 6.6 tons of cocaine aboard the Miami-bound *Limerick*, a Honduran-flag ship. Cuba turned over the cocaine to the United States and cooperated fully in the investigation and subsequent prosecution of two defendants in the case in the United States. Cooperation has increased since 1999 when U.S. and Cuban officials met in Havana to discuss ways of improving anti-drug cooperation. Cuba accepted an upgrading of the communications link between the Cuban Border Guard and the U.S. Coast Guard as well as the stationing of a U.S. Coast Guard Drug Interdiction Specialist (DIS) at the U.S. Interests Section in Havana. The Coast Guard official was posted to the U.S. Interests Section in September 2000, and since that time, coordination has increased.

According to the 2014 *INCSR*, the Coast Guard shares tactical information related to narcotics trafficking on a case by case basis, and responds to Cuban information on vessels transiting through Cuban territorial seas suspected of smuggling. The report maintained that law enforcement communication gradually increased in frequency and transparency in 2013, especially concerning efforts to target drug trafficking at sea. The United States and Cuba held a "professional exchange between experts" on maritime drug interdiction that included tours of facilities, unit capabilities, and possible future joint coordination.

---

[150] Mimi Whitfield, "U.S. Begins New Multiple-Entry Visa Program for Cuban Visitors," Miami Herald, August 1, 2013; Marc Frank, "Cubans Welcome New U.S. Visa Policy, Government Largely Silent," *Reuters News*, August 2, 2013; and U.S. Department of State, United States Interest Section, Havana, Cuba, "Important Notice: Increase in B-2 Visa Validity," available at http://havana.usint.gov/visa_appointment_information.html.

Cuba maintains that it wants to cooperate with the United States to combat drug trafficking, and on various occasions has called for a bilateral anti-drug cooperation agreement with the United States.[151] In the 2011 *INCSR* (issued in March 2011) the State Department acknowledged that Cuba had presented the U.S. government with a draft bilateral accord for counternarcotics cooperation that is still under review. According to the State Department in the *INCSR*: "Structured appropriately, such an accord could advance the counternarcotics efforts undertaken by both countries." The report maintained that greater cooperation among the United States, Cuba, and its international partners—especially in the area of real-time tactical information-sharing and improved tactics, techniques, and procedures—would likely lead to increased interdictions and disruptions of illegal trafficking. These positive U.S. statements regarding a potential bilateral anti-drug cooperation agreement and greater multilateral cooperation in the region with Cuba were reiterated in the 2012, 2013, and 2014 *INCSRs*.

At a February 1, 2012, hearing before the Senate Caucus on International Narcotics Control on U.S.-Caribbean security cooperation, Caucus Chairman Senator Dianne Feinstein stated that "this limited cooperation we do have between our Coast Guard and Cuban authorities has been very useful, and I hope we can find ways to increase our counternarcotics cooperation with Cuba."[152] The caucus released a report on September 13, 2012, in which Senator Feinstein recommended that the Obama Administration consider taking four steps to increase U.S. collaboration with Cuba on counternarcotics: (1) expand the U.S. Coast Guard and law enforcement presence at the U.S. Interests Section in Havana; (2) establish protocols for direct ship-to-ship communication between the U.S. Coast Guard and the Cuban Border Guard; (3) negotiate a bilateral counternarcotics agreement with Cuba; and (4) allow for Cuba's participation in the U.S.-Caribbean Security Dialogue.[153]

Cuba's Offshore Oil Development

Cuba is working toward potential development of its offshore oil resources, but it suffered setbacks in 2012 when three attempts by foreign oil companies drilling wells were unsuccessful. While the country has proven oil reserves of just 0.1 billion barrels, the U.S. Geological Survey estimates that offshore reserves in the North Cuba Basin could contain an additional 4.6 billion barrels of undiscovered technically recoverable crude oil. If oil is found, some experts estimate that it would take at least three to five years before production would begin.

While it is unclear whether offshore oil production could result in Cuba becoming a net oil exporter, it could reduce Cuba's current dependence on Venezuela for oil supplies. As noted above, Venezuela provides Cuba with some 100,000 barrels of oil per day. In 2012, Cuba produced 51,000 barrels of oil per day on its own, with most production occurring onshore, and

---

[151] On March 12, 2002, Cuba's Ministry of Foreign Affairs and the Cuban Interests Section in Washington delivered three diplomatic notes to the U.S. Interests Section in Havana and the State Department in Washington proposing agreements on drug interdiction, terrorism, and migration issues. See "Statement from the Ministry of Foreign Affairs: Prominent Drug Trafficker Arrested in our Country," Information Office, Cuban Interests Section, March 17, 2002; "Cuba Offers to Sign Anti-Drug Pact," *Miami Herald*, April 8, 2006.

[152] "Senate Caucus on International Narcotics Control Holds Hearing on Drug-Related Violence in the Caribbean and U.S. Security Assistance Through the Caribbean Basin Security Initiative," *CQ Congressional Transcripts*, February 1, 2012.

[153] U.S. Congress, Senate United States Senate Caucus on International Narcotics Control, *Preventing a Security Crisis in the Caribbean*, 112th Cong., 2nd sess., September 2012, pp. 38-40, available at http://www.feinstein.senate.gov/public/index.cfm/files/serve/?File_id=90bb66bc-3371-4898-8415-fbfc31c0ed24.

---

consumed 171,000 barrels of oil per day, according to the U.S. Energy Information Administration.[154]

Cuba has had seven offshore deepwater oil projects involving nine foreign companies in 22 exploration blocs. (See **Figure 7** for a map of Cuba's offshore oil blocks.) The Spanish oil company Repsol, in a consortium with Norway's Statoil and India's Oil and Natural Gas Corporation, began offshore exploratory drilling in late January 2012, using an oil rig known as the Scarabeo-9 (owned by an Italian oil services provider, Saipem, a subsidiary of the Italian oil company ENI). On May 18, 2012, however, Repsol announced that its exploratory well came up dry, and the company subsequently announced in late May that it would likely leave Cuba (this was ultimately confirmed by the company in October 2013). In late May 2012, the Scarabeo-9 oil rig was used by the Malaysian company Petronas in cooperation with the Russian company Gazprom to explore for oil in a block off the coast of western Cuba. On August 6, 2012, however, Cuba announced that that the well was found not to be commercially viable because of its compact geological formation. In early September 2012, the Venezuelan oil company, PdVSA, announced that it had started exploring for oil off the coast of western Cuba, but on November 2, 2012, Cuba announced that the well was not commercially viable. In addition to these projects, Cuba has three additional offshore projects with foreign oil companies—PetroVietnam, Sonangol (Angola), and ONGC (India).

As a result of the three unsuccessful wells, the Scarabeo-9 oil rig left Cuba on November 14, 2012, reportedly headed to West Africa. Some oil experts maintain that it could be years before companies decide to return to drill again in Cuba's offshore deepwaters.[155] Most observers maintain that the failure to discover oil in the three wells drilled by the Scrrabeo-9 oil rig in 2012 is a significant setback for the Cuban government's efforts to develop its deepwater offshore hydrocarbon resources.[156]

In December 2012, the Russian energy company, Zarubezhneft, announced that it had begun drilling an exploratory oil well in a north coastal block (in shallow waters, not deepwater exploration) east of Havana off Cayo Coco, a Cuban tourist resort area, and expected to be completed by June 2013.[157] Because of technical problems with the rig and difficult geology, however, the oil rig being used (known as the Songa Mercur operated by Songa Offshore, a Norwegian oil rig company) stopped work in early April 2013 and was redeployed to Asia on June 1, 2013, effectively ending offshore drilling in Cuba for now.[158]

---

[154] U.S. Energy Information Administration, "Country Analysis Note: Cuba," November 2013.

[155] Jeff Franks, "Drilling Rig Leave Cuba, Taking Oil Hopes With It," Reuters News, November 14, 2012, Peter Orsi, "Cuba Says 3rd Deep-Water Oil Well Sunk This Year Not Commercially Viable," *AP Newswire*, November 2, 2012.

[156] "Cuba Offshore Oil Search Fails for a Third Time," *Agence France Presse*, November 2, 2012; "PdVSA Has Third Dry Well in Cuba Deepwater Exploration: Report," *Platts Commodity News*, November 2, 2012.

[157] "Russia's Zarubezhneft Drills Exploration Well in Cuban Offshore Block L," *Platts Commodity News*, December 19, 2012.

[158] "Russian Offshore Drilling to End Earlier than Anticipated," *Cubastandard.com*, April 19, 2013; and "Zarubezhneft Halts Cuba Drilling," *The Oil Daily*, April 24, 2003; "Zurubezhneft Gives Up Drilling Effort Off Cuba's Coast," *Moscow Times*, June 4, 2013.

Figure 7. Cuba's Offshore Oil Blocks

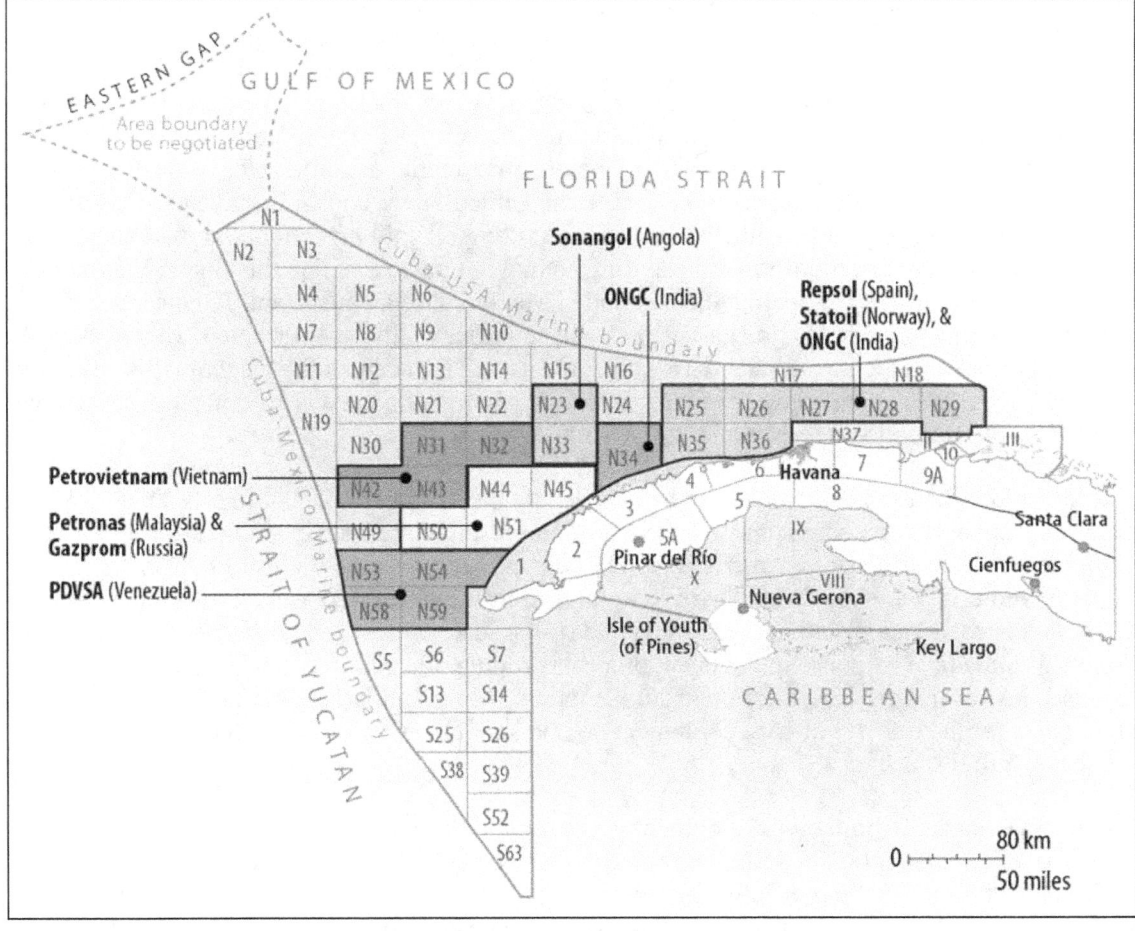

Source: Originally adapted by CRS from Jorge R. Piñon, presentation given at the Inter-American Dialogue, Washington, DC, October 8, 2010. Subsequently updated by CRS.

Notes: Petrobras (Brazil) signed an agreement for exploration of block N37 in October 2008, but announced its withdrawal in March 2011. The China National Petroleum Corporation (CNPC) had been reported in the past to be negotiating several offshore blocks, N19-N22 and N30.

In the aftermath of the Deepwater Horizon oil spill in the Gulf of Mexico, some Members of Congress and others expressed concern about Cuba's development of its deepwater petroleum reserves so close to the United States. They were concerned about oil spill risks and about the status of disaster preparedness and coordination with the United States in the event of an oil spill. Dealing with these challenges is made more difficult because of the long-standing poor state of relations between Cuba and the United States. If an oil spill did occur in the waters northwest of Cuba, currents in the Florida Straits could carry the oil to U.S. waters and coastal areas in Florida, although a number of factors would determine the potential environmental impact. If significant amounts of oil did reach U.S. waters, marine and coastal resources in southern Florida could be at risk.

The final report of the National Commission on the BP Deepwater Horizon Oil Spill and Offshore Drilling, issued in January 2011, maintained that since Mexico already drills in the Gulf of Mexico and Cuba has expressed an interest in deepwater drilling in the Gulf of Mexico, that it is in the U.S. national interest to negotiate with these countries to agree on a common, rigorous set of standards, a system of regulatory oversight, and operator adherence to an effective safety culture, along with protocols to cooperate on containment and response strategies in case of a spill.[159]

With regard to disaster response coordination, while the United States and Cuba are not parties to a bilateral agreement on oil spills, both countries are signatories to multilateral agreements that commit the two parties to prepare for and cooperate on potential oil spills. Under the auspices of the International Maritime Organization (IMO), the United States and Cuba have participated in regional meetings every few months since 2011 regarding oil spill prevention, preparedness, and response that have allowed information sharing among nations, including the United States and Cuba. Other countries participating have included Mexico, the Bahamas, and Jamaica. After numerous rounds of meetings, in March 2014, the countries finalized a document known as the Wider Caribbean Region Multilateral Technical Operating Procedures for Offshore Oil Pollution Response (MTOP), which consists of information of what would need to be done and coordinated in the case of international response to an oil spill.[160]

U.S. oil spill mitigation companies can be licensed by the Treasury and Commerce Departments to provide support and equipment in the event of an oil spill. One such example is a Florida-based company, Clean Caribbean & Americas, which has had licenses to be involved in Cuba since 2001. In addition, the U.S. Coast Guard has obtained licenses from Treasury and Commerce that allow it "to broadly engage in preparedness and response activities, and positions" the agency "to direct an immediate response in the event of a catastrophic oil spill."[161] Some energy and policy analysts, however, have called for the Administration to ease regulatory restrictions on private companies for the transfer of U.S. equipment and personnel to Cuba needed to prevent and combat a spill if it occurs.

Interest in Cuba's offshore oil development was strong in the 112th Congress, particularly over concerns about a potential oil spill, with three congressional hearings held and eight legislative initiatives introduced taking different approaches, none of which were enacted. The various policy approaches included sanctioning foreign companies investing in or supporting Cuba's oil development; requiring the Secretary of the Interior to make recommendations on a joint contingency plan with Mexico, Cuba, and the Bahamas to ensure an adequate response to oil spills; and authorizing U.S. companies to engage in oil spill prevention and clean-up activities in Cuba's offshore oil sector as well as broader exploration and extraction activities.

---

[159] National Commission on the BP Deepwater Horizon Oil Spill and Offshore Drilling, *Deepwater, The Gulf Oil Disaster and the Future of Offshore Drilling,* Report to the President, p. 254 and p. 300. See the full text of the report at http://www.oilspillcommission.gov/sites/default/files/documents/DEEPWATER_ReporttothePresident_FINAL.pdf.

[160] International Maritime Organization, Regional Marine Pollution Emergency Information and Training Center for the Wider Caribbean (REMPEITC-Caribe), *Wider Caribbean Region, Multilateral Technical Operating Procedures for Offshore Oil Pollution Response (MTOP),* March 2014, available at http://cep.unep.org/racrempeitc/regional-oprc-plans/Final_MTOP_Public_version.pdf; Paul Guzzo, "U.S., Cuba Join Caribbean Nations in Oil Cleanup Pact," *Tampa Tribune,* March 17, 2014.

[161] U.S. Congress, House Committee on Transportation and Infrastructure, Subcommittee on Coast Guard and Maritime Transportation, *Offshore Drilling in Cuba and the Bahamas: The U.S. Coast Guard's Oil Spill Readiness and Response Planning,* 112th Cong., 2nd sess., January 30, 2012, 112-70 (Washington: GPO, 2012). Testimony of Rear Admiral William Baumgartner, Commander, Seventh District, and Rear Admiral Cari Thomas, Director of Policy Response, U.S. Coast Guard, available at http://republicans.transportation.house.gov/Media/file/TestimonyCGMT/2012-01-30-BaumgartnerThomas.pdf.

Cuban Spies

Since 2000, some 15 individuals, including two U.S. government officials, have been convicted in the United States on charges involving spying for Cuba.[162] In June 2009, the FBI arrested a retired State Department employee and his wife, Walter Kendall Myers and Gwendolyn Steingraber Myers, for spying for Cuba for three decades. The two were accused of acting as agents of the Cuban government and of passing classified information to the Cuban government. In November 2009, the Myerses pled guilty to the spying charges, and in July 2010 Kendall Myers was sentenced to life in prison while Gwendolyn Myers was sentenced to 81 months.[163]

In 2006, Florida International University (FBI) professor Carlos Alvarez pled guilty to conspiring to be an unregistered agent who had reported on the Cuban exile community, while his wife Elsa Prieto Alvarez, an FIU counselor, pled guilty to being aware of and failing to disclose her husband's activities. Carlos Alvarez received a five-year sentence, while his wife received three years.

In May 2003, the Bush Administration ordered the expulsion of 14 Cuban diplomats (7 from New York and 7 from Washington, DC), maintaining that they were involved in monitoring and surveillance activities.[164] The U.S. intelligence community reportedly had been incensed that Cuba's spies had been stealing information on preparations for the U.S. invasion of Iraq and passing them to the Iraqi government.[165]

On September 21, 2001, Defense Intelligence Agency (DIA) analyst Ana Montes was arrested on charges of spying for the Cuban government. Montes reportedly supplied Cuba with classified information about U.S. military exercises and other sensitive operations.[166] Montes ultimately pled guilty to spying for the Cuban government for 16 years, during which she divulged the names of four U.S. government intelligence agents working in Cuba and information about a "special access program" related to U.S. national defense. She was sentenced in October 2002 to 25 years in prison in exchange for her cooperation with prosecutors as part of a plea bargain. In response to the espionage case, the State Department ordered the expulsion of four Cuban diplomats (two from Cuba's U.N. Mission in New York and two from the Cuban Interests Section in Washington, DC) in November 2002.

In another case related to that of Ana Montes, in April 2013, the Department of Justice unsealed a 2004 indictment charging a former USAID official, Marta Rita Velazquez, with espionage stemming from her role in introducing Montes to the Cuban Intelligence Service in 1984, facilitating Montes's recruitment by Cuban intelligence, and helping Montes gain employment at the DIA. Velazquez joined USAID in 1989 serving as a legal office with responsibilities

---

[162] For background, see Stéphane Lefebvre, "Cuban Intelligence Activities Directed at the United States, 1959-2007," *International Journal of Intelligence and Counterintelligence*, June 2009.

[163] Del Quentin Wilber, "Former U.S. Official, Wife Admit to 30 Years of Spying for Cuba," *Washington Post*, November 21, 2009; and Spencer S. Hsu, "Man Who Spied for Cuba Gets Life," *Washington Post*, July 18, 2010.

[164] "U.S. Orders Expulsion of 14 Cuban Diplomats," *Dow Jones International News*, May 13, 2003; Juan O. Tamayo, "Names of 7 Expelled Cuban Spies Revealed," *Miami Herald*, September 21, 2011.

[165] Juan O Tamayo, "Names of 7 Expelled Cuban Spies Revealed; The U.S. Had Kept Secret the Names of Seven Alleged Cuban Spies Who Were Expelled in 2003," *Miami Herald*, September 21, 2011.

[166] Bill Miller and Walter Pincus, "Defense Analyst Accused of Spying for Cuba," "Woman Passed Classified Information on Military Exercises, FBI Says," *Washington Post*, September 22, 2001.

encompassing Central America, and was also posted to U.S. Embassies in Nicaragua and Guatemala.[167] She resigned from USAID in June 2002 when it was announced that Montes had pled guilty, and moved to Sweden where she remains.[168]

Cuban Five—Now Three

In June 2001, five members of the so-called "Wasp Network" originally arrested in September 1998 were convicted on espionage charges by a U.S. Federal Court in Miami.[169] Sentences handed down for the "Cuban five" in December 2001 ranged from 15 years to life in prison for three of the five. The group of five Cuban intelligence agents—Gerardo Hernández, Ramón Labañino, Antonio Guerrero, Fernando González, and René González—penetrated Cuban exile groups and tried to infiltrate U.S. military bases.

All five were convicted for various offenses, including acting and conspiring to act as unregistered Cuban intelligence agents in the United States; fraud and misuse of identity documents; and in the case of three (Hernández, Labañino, and Guerrero), conspiracy to gather and transmit national defense information. The five did not deny acting as unregistered Cuban agents, but maintain that their role was to focus on Cuban exile groups responsible for hostile acts against Cuba and potential signs of U.S. military action against Cuba.[170]

Gerardo Hernández, who received two life sentences, also was convicted for conspiracy to commit murder for the alleged role he played in the deaths of four pilots of the Cuban American group, Brothers to the Rescue (BTTR), when two small planes they were flying were shot down by the Cuban Air Force in February 1996. The group was known primarily for its humanitarian mission of spotting Cubans fleeing their island nation on rafts, but had also become active in flying over Cuba and dropping anti-government leaflets.

The Cuban government vowed to work for the return of the "Cuban five," who have been dubbed "Heroes of the Republic" by Cuba's National Assembly.[171] In December 2008, Cuban President Raúl Castro offered to exchange some imprisoned Cuban political dissidents for the "Cuban five," an offer that was rejected by the State Department, which maintained that the dissidents should be released immediately without any conditions.

In June 2009, the U.S. Supreme Court chose not to hear an appeal of the case of the "Cuban five" in which their lawyers were asking for a new trial outside Miami before an unbiased jury. Later in 2009, however, sentences for three of the five were reduced: Ramón Labañino had his life

---

[167] U.S. Department of Justice, Office of Public Affairs, "Unsealed Indictment Charges Former U.S. Federal Employee with Conspiracy to Commit Espionage for Cuba," April 25, 2013.

[168] Scott Stewart, "The Cuban Spy Network in the U.S. Government," *Stratfor*, May 2, 2013.

[169] The "Wasp Network (*La Red Avispa*) was a spy ring that operated in South Florida since 1992 under the direction of Cuban's foreign intelligence service. Five additional members of the ring—all U.S. citizens—were convicted in 2000 on lesser charges, with sentences ranging from three and one-half years to seven years (Lefebvre, op. cit.). Another 20 members of the "Wasp network" reportedly were able to escape to Cuba before they could be arrested or went underground in the United States (Brian Latell, *Castro's Secrets, The CIA and Cuba's Intelligence Machine*, New York: Palgrave MacMillan, 2012, pp. 70-71).

[170] Amnesty International, *USA, The Case of the "Cuban Five,"* 2010.

[171] Cuba has also led an international campaign to call attention to the "Cuban five," and exert pressure on the United States for their release. In the United States, the National Committee to Free the Cuban Five organizes events and conducts media campaigns; the group's website is available at http://www.freethefive.org/.

sentence reduced to 30 years; Antonio Guerrero had his life sentence reduced to 21 years and 10 months; and Fernando González had his 19-year sentence reduced to 17 years and 9 months. The sentence of two life terms for Gerardo Hernández, however, was not reduced.

To date, two of the "Cuban five" have been released from prison after serving their sentences (with time off for good behavior) and returned to Cuba. René González, who received a 15-year sentence, was released from prison in October 2011 because of time off for good behavior, but still faced three years of probation; a judge ruled that he had to serve it in the United States. In March 2012, González was allowed by a federal judge in Florida to visit his dying brother in Cuba for a period of two weeks, after which he returned to the United States. González was permitted to return to Cuba on April 22, 2013, for a period of two weeks in the aftermath of his father's death, but a U.S. federal judge ruled in early May 2003 that González could stay in Cuba if he renounced his U.S. citizenship (he was a dual national), which he subsequently did at the U.S. Interests Section in Havana. Fernando González was released on February 27, 2014, and was swiftly returned to Cuba a day later, where he received a hero's welcome. Of the three remaining members of the "Cuban five," Antonio Guerrero and Ramón Labañino potentially could be released in 2017 and 2024, respectively, while Gerardo Hernández continues to face two life terms.

In 2012, Cuba began linking the release of the "Cuban five" to the release of Alan Gross, the U.S. government subcontractor detained in 2009 and sentenced to 15 years in prison for his work on U.S. government-sponsored democracy projects. The United States has rejected such linkages, maintaining there is no equivalence between the cases,[172] and U.S. officials have repeatedly called for Gross's release on humanitarian grounds. (Also see "Imprisonment of USAID Subcontractor since December 2009" above.)

Legislative Initiatives in the 113th Congress

For information on legislative initiatives on Cuba in the 112th Congress, see CRS Report R41617, *Cuba: Issues for the 112th Congress.*

Enacted Measures

P.L. 113-6 (H.R. 933). Consolidated and Further Continuing Appropriations Act, 2013. Provides continued funding for Cuba democracy and human rights projects and Cuba broadcasting (Radio and TV Martí) for FY2013. Signed into law March 26, 2013.

P.L. 113-76 (H.R. 3547). Consolidated Appropriations Act, 2014. (Joint explanatory statement available from the House Committee on Rules, http://rules.house.gov/bill/113/hr-3547-sa). Signed into law January 17, 2014. Provides funding for Cuba democracy and human rights projects and Cuba broadcasting (Radio and TV Martí) for FY2014. With regard to democracy and human rights funding, Division K, Title VII, Section 7045(b) of the law provides up to $17.5 million in Economic Support Funds (ESF) for programs and activities in Cuba and stipulates that no ESF appropriated under the Act may be obligated by USAID for any new programs or activities in

---

[172] U.S. Department of State, Daily Press Briefing, May 11, 2012, available at http://www.state.gov/r/pa/prs/dpb/2012/05/189753.htm.

Cuba. The joint explanatory statement to the bill states that of the $17.5 million, not less than $7.5 million shall be provided directly to the National Endowment for Democracy, and not more than $10 million shall be administered by the State Department's Bureau of Democracy, Human Rights, and Labor and Bureau of Western Hemisphere Affairs. With regard to Cuba broadcasting, the joint explanatory statement provides (pursuant to Section 7019 of the law) $27.043 million. Also see H.R. 2786, S. 1371, H.R. 2855, and S. 1372 below.

Additional Measures

H.R. 214 (Serrano). Cuba Reconciliation Act. Would lift the trade embargo on Cuba. Introduced January 4, 2013; referred to the Committee on Foreign Affairs, and in addition to the Committees on Ways and Means, Energy and Commerce, Financial Services, the Judiciary, Oversight and Government Reform, and Agriculture.

H.R. 215 (Serrano). Baseball Diplomacy Act. Would waive certain prohibitions with respect to nationals of Cuba coming to the United States to play organized professional baseball. Introduced January 4, 2013; referred to the Committee on Foreign Affairs, and in addition to the Committee on the Judiciary.

H.R. 778 (Issa)/S. 647 (Nelson). No Stolen Trademarks Honored in America Act. Identical bills would modify a 1998 prohibition (Section 211 of Division A, Title II, P.L. 105-277) by U.S. courts of certain rights relating to certain marks, trade names, or commercial names. The 1998 prohibition or sanction prevents trademark registrations and renewals from Cuban or foreign nations that were used in connection with a business or assets in Cuba that were confiscated, without the consent of the original owner. The bill would apply a fix so that the sanction would apply to all nationals and would bring the sanction into compliance with a 2002 World Trade Organization dispute settlement ruling. H.R. 778 introduced February 15, 2013; referred to the Committee on the Judiciary. S. 647 introduced March 21, 2013; referred to the Committee on the Judiciary.

H.R. 871 (Rangel). Export Freedom to Cuba Act of 2013. Would allow travel between the United States and Cuba. Introduced February 27, 2013; referred to the Committee on Foreign Affairs.

H.R. 872 (Rangel). Free Trade with Cuba Act. Would lift the trade embargo on Cuba. Introduced February 27, 2013; referred to the Committee on Foreign Affairs, and in addition to the Committees on Ways and Means, Energy and Commerce, the Judiciary, Financial Services, Oversight and Government Reform, and Agriculture.

H.R. 873 (Rangel). Promoting American Agriculture and Medical Exports to Cuba Act of 2013. Would facilitate the export of U.S. agricultural products to Cuba, remove impediments to the export of medical devices and medicines to Cuba, allow travel to Cuba by U.S. legal residents, and establish an agricultural export promotion program with respect to Cuba. Introduced February 27, 2013; referred to the Committee on Foreign Affairs, and in addition to the Committees on Ways and Means, the Judiciary, Agriculture, and Financial Services.

H.R. 1917 (Rush). United States-Cuba Normalization Act of 2013. The bill would lift the U.S. trade embargo on Cuba; repeal a 1998 trademark sanction (Section 211 of Division A, Title II, P.L. 105-277); prohibit restrictions on travel to Cuba; call on the President to conduct negotiations with Cuba to settle property claims of U.S. nationals for confiscated property and secure the protection of internationally recognized human rights; extend nondiscriminatory trade treatment to the products of Cuba; prohibit any limitations on annual remittances to Cuba; remove Cuba from the state sponsors of terrorism list; and call for the immediate and unconditional release of Alan Gross and, until then, urge Cuba to allow Mr. Gross to choose a doctor to provide him with an independent medical assessment. The amendments made by this Act would take effect 60 days after its enactment or 60 days after the President certifies to Congress that Alan Gross has been released by Cuba, whichever occurs later. Introduced May 9, 2013; referred to the Committee on Foreign Affairs, and in addition to the Committees on Ways and Means, Energy and Commerce, the Judiciary, Financial Services, Oversight and Government Reform, and Agriculture.

H.R. 2786 (Crenshaw)/ S. 1371 (Udall, NM). FY2014 Financial Services and General Government Appropriations Act. Both bills had contrasting provisions regarding U.S. travel to Cuba, but none of these provisions were included in the FY2014 omnibus appropriations measure, P.L. 113-76, noted above.

H.R. 2786 introduced and reported by the House Appropriations Committee (H.Rept. 113-172) July 23, 2013. Section 124 would have prohibited FY2014 funding used "to approve, license, facilitate, authorize, or otherwise allow" travel-related or other transactions related to nonacademic educational exchanges (i.e. people-to-people travel) to Cuba set forth in 31 C.F.R. 515.565(b)(2) of the CACR. Section 125 of the House bill would have required a Treasury Department report within 90 days of the bill's enactment with information for each fiscal year since FY2007 on the number of travelers visiting close relatives in Cuba; the average duration of these trips; the average amount of U.S. dollars spent per family traveler (including amount of remittances carried to Cuba); the number of return trips per year; and the total sum of U.S. dollars spent collectively by family travelers for each fiscal year.

S. 1371 introduced and reported by the Senate Appropriations Committee (S.Rept. 113-80) July 25, 2013. Section 628 would have provided for a new general license for travel-related transactions for full-time professional research; attendance at professional meetings if the sponsoring organization was a U.S. organization; and the organization and management of professional meetings and conferences in Cuba if the sponsoring organization was a U.S. professional organization – *if* the travel was related to disaster prevention, emergency preparedness, and natural resource protection, including for fisheries, coral reefs, and migratory species.

H.R. 2855 (Granger)/S. 1372 (Leahy). FY2014 Department of State, Foreign Operations, and Related Programs Appropriations Act. H.R. 2855 introduced and reported (H.Rept. 113-185) July 30, 2013. S. 1372 introduced and reported (S.Rept. 113-81) July 25, 2013. The House version would have provided that $20 million in ESF assistance ($5 million more than the Administration's request) be transferred to the National Endowment for Democracy "to promote democracy and strengthen civil society in Cuba," while the Senate version would have provided that ESF assistance appropriated for Cuba only be made available "for humanitarian assistance and to support the development of private business." The House version would also have provided $28.266 million for Cuba broadcasting (Radio and TV Martí), while S. 1372 would have provided $23.804 million, the same amount as the Administration's request. For final action, see the FY2014 omnibus appropriations measure, P.L. 113-76, described above.

H.R. 3585 (Smith, NJ). Walter Patterson and Werner Foerster Justice and Extradition Act. Would require the President, within 270 days after enactment of the Act and each year after that, to submit a report to the appropriated congressional committees on fugitives currently residing in other countries whose extradition is sought by the United States. Introduced November 21, 2013; referred to the House Committee on Foreign Affairs.

H.R. 4194 (Issa)/ S. 2109 (Warner)/. Government Reports Elimination Act of 2014. Section 1501 of the House bill and Section 2413 of the Senate bill would repeal a reporting requirement regarding commerce with, and assistance to, Cuba from other foreign countries set forth in Section 108 of the Cuban Liberty and Democratic Solidarity Act of 1996 (22 U.S.C. 6038). H.R. 4194 introduced March 11, 2014; reported by the House Committee on Oversight and Government Reform (H.Rept. 113-419) and passed House by voice vote April 28, 2014. S. 2109 introduced March 11, 2014; referred to the Committee on Homeland Security and Governmental Affairs.

H.Res. 121 (Hastings, FL). Would honor Cuban blogger Yoani Sánchez "for her ongoing efforts to challenge political, economic, and social oppression by the Castro regime." Introduced March 15, 2013; referred to the Committee on Foreign Affairs and in addition to the Committee on the Judiciary.

H.Res. 262 (King, NY). Would call for the immediate extradition or rendering to the United States of convicted felon William Morales and all other fugitives from justice who are receiving safe harbor in Cuba in order to escape prosecution or confinement for criminal offenses committed in the United States. Introduced June 14, 2013; referred to the Committee on Foreign Affairs.

S. 1681(Feinstein). Intelligence Authorization Act for Fiscal Year 2014. Section 325 of the bill would repeal a reporting requirement on commerce with, and assistance to, Cuba from other foreign countries set forth in Section 108 of the Cuban Liberty and Democratic Solidarity Act of 1996 (22 U.S.C. 6038). Introduced November 12, 2013; reported by Select Committee on Intelligence November 13, 2013 (S.Rept. 113-120).

Appendix A. Selected Executive Branch Reports and Web Pages

U.S. Relations with Cuba, Fact Sheet, State Department
Date: August 30, 2013
Full Text: http://www.state.gov/r/pa/ei/bgn/2886.htm

Congressional Budget Justification, Department of State, Foreign Operations and Related Programs, FY2015, State Department
Date: March 4, 2014
Full Text: http://www.state.gov/documents/organization/222898.pdf

Congressional Budget Justification for Foreign Operations FY2015, Annex 3: Regional Perspectives (pp.646-647), State Department
Date: April 18, 2014
Full Text: http://www.state.gov/documents/organization/224070.pdf

Country Reports on Human Rights Practices 2013, Cuba, State Department
Date: February 27, 2014
Full Text: http://www.state.gov/documents/organization/220646.pdf

Country Reports on Terrorism 2013 (State Sponsors of Terrorism chapter), State Department
Date: April 2014
Full Text: http://www.state.gov/j/ct/rls/crt/2013/224826.htm

Cuba Country Page, State Department
Full Text: http://www.state.gov/p/wha/ci/cu/

Cuba Country Page, U.S. Agency for International Development
Full Text: http://www.usaid.gov/where-we-work/latin-american-and-caribbean/cuba

Cuba Sanctions, Treasury Department
Full Text: http://www.treasury.gov/resource-center/sanctions/Programs/pages/cuba.aspx

Cuba: What You Need to Know About U.S. Sanctions Against Cuba, Treasury Department, Office of Foreign Assets Control
Date: January 24, 2012
Full Text: http://www.treasury.gov/resource-center/sanctions/Programs/Documents/cuba.pdf

International Religious Freedom Report, 2011, Cuba, State Department
Date: May 20, 2013
Full Text: http://www.state.gov/documents/organization/208682.pdf

International Narcotics Control Strategy Report 2014, Vol. I, Cuba, State Department
Date: March 2014
Full Text: http://www.state.gov/j/inl/rls/nrcrpt/2014/vol1/222869.htm

Trafficking in Persons Report 2012 (Cuba, pp. 144-145 of pdf), State Department
Date: June 19, 2013
Full Text: http://www.state.gov/documents/organization/210738.pdf

Appendix B. Earlier Developments in 2013

On January 28-29, 2014, Cuba hosted the second annual summit of the Community of Latin American and Caribbean Nations (CELAC). The U.N. Secretary General attended and reportedly raised human rights issues with Cuban officials. In a joint declaration, Latin American nations committed to nonintervention and pledged to respect "the inalienable right of every state to choose its political, economic, social, and cultural system."

On January 17, 2014, President Obama signed into law the FY2014 omnibus appropriation measure, H.R. 3547 (P.L. 113-76), which stated that up to $17.5 million should be provided for democracy and human rights programs and activities in Cuba and $27.043 million for Cuba broadcasting (Radio and TV Martí). The measure did not include any provisions tightening or easing U.S. restrictions on travel to Cuba that had been in the House and Senate versions of the FY2014 Financial Services appropriations bill, H.R. 2786 and S. 1371, respectively.

On January 9, 2014, U.S. and Cuban officials met in Havana for semi-annual migration talks. The U.S. delegation again raised the issue of Cuba's continued imprisonment of Alan Gross.

On December 10, 2013, a handshake between President Obama and President Raúl Castro at the memorial service for Nelson Mandela in South Africa generated considerable international press attention.

On December 10, 2013, Cuba cracked down on protests and gatherings planned to commemorate International Human Rights Day and detained more than 150 dissidents.

On December 9, 2013, Cuba announced that it had temporarily reopened its consular services in the United States after the New York-based M&T Bank postponed closing the accounts of Cuba's diplomatic missions in Washington, DC and New York until March 1, 2014. Cuba had suspended its U.S. consular services on November 26 because M&T Bank had decided to stop offering banking services to Cuba's diplomatic missions in the United States. Cuba is continuing to search for a replacement for M&T Bank.

On November 18, 2013, in remarks at the Organization of American States, Secretary of State John Kerry maintained that the United States and Cuba "are finding some cooperation on common interests at this point in time" and noted that the Administration welcomes "some of the changes that are taking place in Cuba." However, the Secretary also cautioned that changes in Cuba "should absolutely not blind us to the authoritarian reality of life for ordinary Cubans."

On November 8, 2013 in Miami, Florida, President Obama stated, in commenting about U.S. policy toward Cuba, that "we have to be creative ... we have to be thoughtful ... and we have to continue to update our policies."

On October 22, 2013, Cuba announced that it would move toward ending its dual-currency system and move toward monetary unification, although it did not provide details or a timetable for the process.

On September 26, 2013, the House Foreign Affairs Committee's Subcommittee on the Western Hemisphere held a hearing on Panama's July 2013 interdiction of a North Korean ship, the *Chong Chon Gang*, that had made stops in Cuba and was found to have weapons hidden aboard on its way back to North Korea.

On September 23, 2013, prominent dissident economist Oscar Espinosa Chepe died in Spain after battling chronic liver disease and cancer.

On September 20, 2013, the United States and Cuba reached a preliminary agreement on air and maritime search and rescue.

On September 16-17, 2013, the United States and Cuba held talks in Havana on restoring direct mail service that had been curtailed in the early 1960s. Talks also were held in Washington D.C. on June 18-19, 2013.

On September 15, 2013, Cuba's Conference of Catholic Bishops issued a pastoral letter maintaining that Cuba's political order needed to be updated and that there should be the right of diversity with respect to thought.

On August 2, 2013, Cuban human rights activist Iván Fernández Depestre, who had been arrested on July 30 after participating in a peaceful protest, was convicted of "dangerousness" in a summary trial and sentenced to three years in prison. Amnesty International considers him a prisoner of conscience along with five other imprisoned Cubans.

On August 1, 2013, the State Department made non-immigrant visas issued to Cubans for family visits, tourism, medical treatment, or other personal travel valid for five years with multiple entries (instead of single entry for six months).

On July 17, 2013, the United States and Cuba held migration talks in Washington D.C. with both sides issuing positive statements after the meeting; the last round of migration talks had been in January 2011.

On June 1, 2013, an oil rig that had been drilling an exploratory well in a north coastal block east of Havana for the Russian energy company Zarubezhneft was redeployed to Asia. Zarubezhneft said that it experience technical problems with the rig and difficult geology in the area. The action effectively ended offshore drilling in Cuba for now, although Zarubezhneft contends that it will return next year to drill in Cuba.

On May 30, 2013, the State Department issued its *Country Reports on Terrorism 2012* report, which provides information related to Cuba being on the department's state sponsors of terrorism list. In the report, the State Department stated that there was no indication that the Cuban government provided weapons or paramilitary training to terrorist groups, but it noted that Cuba continues to provide safe haven to some members of the Basque Fatherland and Liberty (ETA) terrorist group as well as U.S. fugitives from justice.

On May 16, 2013, imprisoned U.S. Agency for International Development subcontractor Alan Gross reached an undisclosed settlement against his employer, Development Alternatives Inc. Gross and his wife had filed suit in November 2012 in U.S. District Court for failing to disclose the risk that he faced while participating in a project in Cuba. Subsequently, on May 28, 2013, a U.S. federal judge dismissed Gross's lawsuit against the U.S. government.

On May 3, 2013, a U.S. federal judge ruled that René González, one of the so-called "Cuban five" spies convicted in the United States in 2001, could stay in Cuba if he renounced his U.S. citizenship, which he subsequently did. González, who had been released from prison in October 2011 but still faced three more years of probation in Florida, had been permitted to visit Cuba for two weeks in the aftermath of his father's death in April 2013.

On April 25, 2013, the Department of Justice unsealed a 2004 indictment charging a former U.S. government official, Marta Rita Velazquez, with espionage stemming from her role in introducing Ana Montes (former U.S. government official who pled guilty in 2002 of spying for Cuba) to the Cuban intelligence service.

On April 19, 2013, the State Department issued its *Country Reports on Human Rights Practices for 2012*, which stated that Cuba's "principal human rights abuses were: abridgement of the rights of citizens to change the government; government threats, intimidation, mobs, harassment, and detentions to prevent free expression and peaceful assembly; and a record number of politically motivated and at times violent short-term detentions."

On April 10, 2013, the State Department released its FY2014 budget request for international programs, which included $15 million in Cuba democracy and human rights projects, $5 million less than appropriated in FY2012. On the same day, the Broadcasting Board of Governors released the details of its FY2014 budget request, including $23.804 million for Cuba broadcasting (Radio and TV Martí), about $4.5 million less than that provided in FY2013, although roughly similar to the FY2013 budget request.

On March 28, 2013, the U.S. Department of State called for an "investigation with independent international observers into the circumstances leading to the death of [Cuban human rights activists] Oswaldo Payá and Harold Cepero" in July 2012.

On March 14, 2013, internationally known Cuban blogger Yoani Sánchez (on a multi-nation trip after receiving a new passport under Cuba's new travel policy) arrived in the United States, with stops in New York City and Washington, DC (including Capitol Hill), through March 21. She then traveled to Europe, but returned to the United States March 28, arriving in Miami.

On March 14, 2013, Amnesty International issued an urgent action appeal for prisoner of conscience Calixto Ramón Martínez Arias who began a hunger strike in early March. Calixto was imprisoned in September 2012 for reporting on a cholera outbreak.

On March 12, 2013, the State Department released its 2013 *International Narcotics Control Strategy Report*, which stated that Cuba maintained a significant level of anti-drug cooperation with the United States in 2012. The report also indicated that the U.S. government was still reviewing a draft bilateral counternarcotics cooperation accord that Cuba presented in 2011, and that such an accord, if structured appropriately, could advance counternarcotics efforts taken by both countries.

On March 6, 2013, the *Washington Post* published an interview with Spanish politician Angel Carromero, who was convicted by a Cuban court in October 2012 for vehicular manslaughter in the death of two human rights activists, including internationally known dissident Oswaldo Payá. Carromero asserted in the interview that the car he was driving was struck from behind and that he had been heavily drugged when he admitted to driving recklessly. Many observers have called for an independent investigation into the accident. In July 2012, the U.S. Senate approved S.Res. 525 (Nelson) calling for an impartial third-party investigation of the crash.

On March 5, 2013, Venezuelan President Hugo Chávez died after battling several recurrences of cancer since mid-2011. Under President Chávez, Venezuela became a strong political and financial supporter of Cuba over the past decade, providing the island with some 100,000 barrels of oil per day.

On February 24, 2013, Cuba's National Assembly, as expected, appointed Raúl Castro to a second five-year term as President. Most significantly, the Assembly also appointed 52-year old Miguel Díaz-Canel as First Vice President, making him Castro's constitutional successor. Díaz-Canel replaced outgoing 82-year old First Vice President José Ramón Machado Ventura.

On January 14, 2013, Cuba's new travel policy went into effect whereby Cubans wanting to travel abroad no longer need an exit permit and letter of invitation. Under the new policy, travel requires only an updated passport and a visa issued by the country of destination, if required. Thousands of Cubans lined up at government migration offices and travel agencies on the first day.

Author Contact Information

Mark P. Sullivan
Specialist in Latin American Affairs
msullivan@crs.loc.gov, 7-7689

Acknowledgments

Susan G. Chesser, Information Research Specialist, produced the statistical figures presented in this report.